GUN RIGHTS AFFIRMED

THE EMERSON CASE

Alan M. Gottlieb

Merril Press
Bellevue, Washington

Gun Rights Affirmed

Published by Merril Press
First Printing August 2001
Second Printing May 2002

Merril Press
Merril Mail Marketing, Inc.
P.O. Box 1682
Bellevue, Washington 98005
Telephone: 425-454-7009

Visit us at our website for additional copies ($10.00 each) of this title and others at www.merrilpress.com

Library of Congress Cataloging-In-Publication Data

Gottlieb, Alan M.
    Gun rights affirmed : the Emerson case / Alan M.
    Gottlieb.
        p. cm.
    Includes bibliographical references.
    ISBN 0-936783-29-X (pbk.)
    1. Emerson, Timothy Joe--Trials litigation, etc. 2. Fire arms--Law and legislation--United States. 3. Gun control --United States. I. Title.

KF224.E48 G68 2000
344.73'0533--dc21

                                00-061086

PRINTED IN THE UNITED STATES OF AMERICA

TABLE OF CONTENTS

INTRODUCTION

By Alan Gottlieb

Federal Judge Sam Cummings of the Northern District of Texas dismissed an indictment against Timothy Joe Emerson for possession of a firearm while having a temporary restraining order against him. The judge cited violations of Emerson's Second and Fifth Amendment rights, and rejected the Government lawyer's claim that it was "well-settled" that the Second Amendment was only a collective right.

This marks the first time in over 60 years that a federal judge has correctly interpreted the Second Amendment as a crucial individual right.

This is one of the strongest rulings I have read regarding any of the Bill of Rights. The overwhelming evidence proving the founding fathers' intent is very meticulously researched and coherently laid out for all to see.

The case arises from a divorce proceeding began by Emerson's wife. The presiding judge issued a temporary restraining order against Dr. Emerson prohibiting him from engaging in various financial transactions (such as emptying the joint accounts), or threatening harm to his wife or her live-in boyfriend.

Mrs. Emerson claimed that Dr. Emerson had made a telephone death threat against her lover. The judge did not issue a finding that Dr. Emerson was a possible danger, nor did he warn Dr. Emerson that he faced possible federal felony prosecution if caught with a firearm (18 U.S.C. § 922(g)(8)) after the restraining order was activated.

Unaware of his prohibited status, Dr. Emerson was later found in possession of a firearm and indicted for this offense. Which brings us to his attempted prosecution in Judge Sam Cummings court-room. Mr. Emerson moved to dismiss the charge as an unconstitutional exercise of congressional power under the Commerce Clause and the Second, Fifth, and Tenth Amendments to the United States Constitution. Judge Cummings agreed to dismiss on violations on Second and Fifth Amendment grounds.

The vast majority of the decision is a discussion of the real meaning of the Second Amendment. Judge Cummings begins by going through the two schools of thought, the "states' rights" or "collective rights" theory versus the "individual rights" theory. Cummings then enumerates in great detail why an individual right, now known as the "Standard Model" in academic literature, is the proper interpretation. Judge Cummings cites as his many reasons for supporting an individual right include:

1. Textual Analysis. The subordinate "Militia" clause, does not negate or limit the independent "the right of the people" clause. Furthermore, the U.S. Supreme Court has determined that "the people" should be interpreted similarly in the First, Second, Fourth, Fifth, and Ninth Amendments.

2. Historical Analysis. Judge Cummings found that an examination of (a) English History, (b) Colonial Right to Bear Arms, (c) The Ratification Debates, and (d) Drafting of the Second Amendment all show clearly that the right was meant as an individual protection. The Judge repeatedly cited relevant English and Colonial laws, quoted from numerous founding fathers, and provided a crucial history lesson on how, "Without that individual right [to bear arms], the colonists never could have won the Revolutionary War."

3. Structural Analysis. The structure of the Second Amendment within the Bill of Rights proves that the right to bear arms is an individual right, rather than

a collective one. Of the first ten amendments to the Constitution, only the Tenth concerns itself with the states, and refers to such powers in addition to, not instead of, individual rights. The Tenth Amendment reads, "The powers not delegated to the United States by the Constitution, nor prohibited by it to the states, are reserved to the states respectively, or to the people."

4. Judicial Interpretations. Judge Cummings notes that the courts have been divided on this issue, and but that the U.S. Supreme Court has not had a true Second Amendment case since 1939.

5. Prudential Concerns. Judge Cummings also admonished people who are trying to eliminate the right to keep and bear arms just because that right is outdated, unpopular, or costly. Such "cost-benefit" analysis merely proves that the founding fathers were right in including it in the Bill of Rights.

Judge Cummings then utilized his skilled reasoning to conclude that the federal unlawful possession law (18 U.S.C. §922(g)(8)), "is unconstitutional because it allows a state court divorce proceeding, without particularized findings of the threat of future violence, to automatically deprive a citizen of his Second Amendment rights. The statute allows, but does not require, that the restraining order include a finding that the person under the order represents a credible threat to the physical safety of the intimate partner or child....Therefore, by criminalizing protected Second Amendment activity based upon a civil state court order with no particularized findings, the statute is over-broad and in direct violation of an individual's Second Amendment rights."

This decision helps protect gun owners from the ever-increasing classes of people prohibited from gun ownership. Without a court willing to step in and put a halt to this practice, eventually anyone with a parking or speeding ticket could be prevented from gun ownership.

This book includes Judge Cumming's ruling and the amicus curi placed before the Fifth Circuit Federal Appellate Court in support of the decision by the Second Amendment Foundation, the Citizens Committee for the Right to Keep and Bear Arms and the National Rifle Association.

The Appellate Court decision in this case made Second Amendment judicial history when it reaffirmed trial Judge Sam Cumming's individual rights decision.

> A well regulated Militia, being necessary to the security of a free State, the right of the people to keep and bear Arms, shall not be infringed.

> U.S. CONST. amend. II.

IN THE UNITED STATES DISTRICT COURT
FOR THE NORTHERN DISTRICT OF TEXAS
SAN ANGELO DIVISION

UNITED STATES OF AMERICA	§	
	§	
	§	Criminal Action No.
v.	§	6:98-CR-103-C
	§	
TIMOTHY JOE EMERSON	§	

AMENDED MEMORANDUM OPINION

[See footnote 1]

Defendant Timothy Joe Emerson ("Emerson") moves to dismiss the Indictment against him, claiming that the statute he is prosecuted under, 18 U.S.C. § 922(g)(8), is an unconstitutional exercise of congressional power under the Commerce Clause and the Second, Fifth, and Tenth Amendments to the United States Constitution. For the reasons stated below, the Court GRANTS Emerson's Motion to Dismiss.

1. BACKGROUND

On August 28, 1998, Emerson's wife, Sacha, filed a petition for divorce and application for a temporary restraining order in the 119th District Court of Tom Green County, Texas. The petition stated no factual basis for relief other than the necessary recitals required under the Texas Family Code regarding domicile, service of process, dates of marriage and separation, and the "insupportability" of the marriage. The application for a temporary restraining order—essentially a form order frequently used in Texas divorce procedure—sought to enjoin Emerson from engaging in various financial transactions to maintain the financial status quo and from making threatening communications or actual attacks upon his wife during the pendency of the divorce proceedings.

On September 4, 1998, the Honorable John E. Sutton held a hearing on Mrs. Emerson's application for a temporary restraining order. Mrs. Emerson was represented by an attorney at that hearing, and Mr. Emerson appeared *pro se*. Mrs. Emerson testified about her economic situation, her needs in the way of temporary spousal support and child support, and her desires regarding temporary conservatorship of their minor child.

During the hearing, Mrs. Emerson alleged that her husband threatened over the telephone to kill the man with whom Mrs. Emerson had been having an adulterous affair. However, no evidence was adduced concerning any acts of violence or threatened violence by Mr. Emerson against any member of his family, and the district court made no findings to that effect. Furthermore, the court did not admonish Mr. Emerson that if he granted the temporary restraining order, Mr. Emerson would be subject to federal criminal prosecution merely for possessing a firearm while being subject to the order.

II. ANALYSIS

As stated above, Emerson was indicted for possession of a firearm while being under a restraining order, in violation of 18 U.S.C. § 922(g)(8) ("the Act"). This statute states that:

(g) It shall be unlawful for any person—
    (8) who is subject to a court order that—
        (A) was issued after a hearing of which such person received actual notice, and at which such person had an opportunity to participate;
        (B) restrains such person from harassing, stalking, or threatening an intimate partner of such person or child of such intimate partner or person, or engaging in other conduct that would place an intimate partner in reasonable fear of

bodily injury to the partner or child; and
(i) includes a finding that such person represents a credible threat to the physical safety
of such intimate partner or child; or
(ii) by its terms explicitly prohibits the use,
attempted use, or threatened use of physical
force against such intimate partner or child
that would reasonably be expected to cause
bodily injury .... 18 U.S.C. § 922(g)(8).

Emerson argues that 18 U.S.C. § 922(g)(8) is an
unconstitutional exercise of congressional power under the Commerce Clause and the Second, Fifth, and
Tenth Amendments to the United States Constitution. The Court will address these arguments *seria-
tim*.

A. Commerce Clause

Emerson first argues that 18 U.S.C. § 922(g)(8) is
an unconstitutional exercise of congressional power
under the Commerce Clause of the United States
Constitution. U.S. CONST. art. I, § 8, cl. 3. Pursuant
to the Supreme Court's holding in *United States v.
Lopez*, 514 U.S. 549 (1995), Emerson argues that the
Act is unconstitutional because it does not regulate
commercial activity.

However, the Fifth Circuit Court of Appeals has
examined the validity of 18 U.S.C. § 922(g)(8) under a
Commerce Clause challenge and has held that the Act
is constitutional. *United States v. Pierson*, 139 F.3d
501 (5th Cir. 1998). Accordingly, Emerson cannot sus-
tain a Motion to Dismiss under a Commerce Clause
challenge.

B. Second Amendment

Emerson claims that 18 U.S.C. § 922(g)(8) violates
his rights under the Second Amendment to the United
States Constitution. The Second Amendment states
that:

A well regulated Militia, being necessary to the security of a free State, the right of the people to keep and bear Arms, shall not be infringed.

U.S. CONST. amend. II.

Only if the Second Amendment guarantees Emerson a personal right to bear arms can he claim a constitutional violation. Whether the Second Amendment recognizes an individual right to keep and bear arms is an issue of first impression within the Fifth Circuit. Emerson claims that he has a personal right to bear arms which the Act infringes, while at oral argument on the Motion to Dismiss, the Government claimed it is "well settled" that the Second Amendment creates a right held by the States and does not protect an individual right to bear arms.

1. SECOND AMENDMENT SCHOOLS OF THOUGHT

Two main schools of thought have developed on the issue of whether the Second Amendment recognizes individual or collective rights. These schools of thought are referred to as the "states' rights," or "collective rights," school and the "individual rights" school. The former group cites the opening phrase of the amendment, along with subsequent case law, as authority for the idea that the right only allows states to establish and maintain militias, and in no way creates or protects an individual right to own arms. David E. Johnson, Note, *Taking a Second Look at the Second Amendment and Modern Gun Control Laws,* 86 KY. L.J. 197, 198 (1997-98) (citing Andrew D. Herz, *Gun Crazy: Constitutional False Consciousness and Dereliction of Dialogic Responsibility,* 75 B.U. L. REV. 57 (1995)). Due to changes in the political climate over the last two centuries and the rise of National Guard organizations among the states, states' rights theorists argue that the Second Amendment is an anachronism, and that there is no longer a need to protect any right to private gun ownership.

The individual rights theorists, supporting what has become known in the academic literature as the "Standard Model," argue that the amendment protects an individual right inherent in the concept of ordered liberty, and resist any attempt to circumscribe such a right. *Id.* (citing Glenn Harlan Reynolds, *A Critical Guide to the Second Amendment,* 62 TENN. L. REV. 461, 464-88 (1995); Robert Dowlut, *The Right to Keep and Bear Arms: A Right to Self-Defense Against Criminals and Despots,* 8 STAN. L. & POL'Y REV. 25 (1997)).

2. TEXTUAL ANALYIS

A textual analysis of the Second Amendment supports an individual right to bear arms. A distinguishing characteristic of the Second Amendment is the inclusion of an opening clause or preamble, which sets out its purpose. No similar clause is found in any other amendment. Stanford Levinson, *The Embarrassing Second Amendment,* 99 YALE L.J. 637, 644 (1989). While states' rights theorists seize upon this first clause to the exclusion of the second, both clauses should be read *in pari materia,* to give effect and harmonize both clauses, rather than construe them as being mutually exclusive.

The amendment reads "[a] well regulated Militia, being necessary to the security of a free State, the right of the people to keep and bear Arms, shall not be infringed." U.S. CONST. amend. II. Within the amendment are two distinct clauses, the first subordinate and the second independent. If the amendment consisted solely of its independent clause, "the right of the people to keep and bear Arms, shall not be infringed," then there would be no question whether the right is individual in nature. David E. Johnson, Note, *Taking a Second Look at the Second Amendment and Modern Gun Control Laws,* 86 KY. L.J. 197, 200 (1997-98).

Collective rights theorists argue that addition of the subordinate clause qualifies the rest of the amendment by placing a limitation on the people's right to bear arms. *Id.* However, if the amendment truly meant what collective rights advocates propose, then the text would read "[a] well <u>regulated</u> Militia, being necessary to the security of a free State, the right of the *States* to keep and bear Arms, shall not be infringed." However, that is not what the framers of the amendment drafted. The plain language of the amendment, without attenuate inferences therefrom, shows that the function of the subordinate clause was not to qualify the right, but instead to show why it must be protected. *Id.* The right exists independent of the existence of the militia. If this right were not protected, the existence of the militia, and consequently the security of the state, would be jeopardized. *Id.* at 201.

The Supreme Court recently interpreted the text of the Second Amendment and noted that the phrase "the people" in the Second Amendment has the same meaning in both the Preamble to the Constitution and in the First, Fourth, Fifth, and Ninth Amendments. *United States v. Verdugo-Urquidez,* 494 U.S. 259, 265 (1990). The Court held that the phrase "the people" "seems to have been a term of art employed in select parts of the Constitution."

<u>The Second Amendment protects "the right of the people to keep and bear Arms," and the Ninth and Tenth Amendments provide that certain rights and powers are retained by and reserved to "the people."</u>

* * *

<u>While this textual exegesis is by no means conclusive, it suggests that "the people" protected by the Fourth Amendment, and by the First and Second Amendments, . . . refers to a class of persons who are part of a national community or who have otherwise developed sufficient connection with this country to be considered part of that community.</u> *See United States ex rel. Turner v. Williams,* 194 U.S. 279, 292 (1904).

The Court has also held that given their contemporaneous proposal and passage, the amendments of the Bill of Rights should be read *in pari materia*, and amendments which contain similar language should be construed similarly. *Patton v. United States,* 281 U.S. 276, 298 (1930), *cited by* David Harmer, *Securing a Free State: Why the Second Amendment Matters,* 1998 BYU L. REV. 55, 61 (1998). The Court's construction of "the people" as used in the Second Amendment supports a holding that the right to keep and bear arms is a personal right retained by the people, as opposed to a collective right held by the States. Thus, a textual analysis of the Second Amendment clearly declares a substantive right to bear arms recognized in the people of the United States.

3. HISTORICAL ANALYSIS

"[T]here is a long tradition of widespread lawful gun ownership by private individuals in this country." *Staples v. United States,* 511 U.S. 600, 610 (1994). A historical examination of the right to bear arms, from English antecedents to the drafting of the Second Amendment, bears proof that the right to bear arms has consistently been, and should still be, construed as an individual right.

a. English History

A review of English history explains the founders' intent in drafting the Second Amendment. As long ago as 690 A.D., Englishmen were required to possess arms and to serve in the military. David T. Hardy, *Armed Citizens, Citizen Armies: Toward a Jurisprudence of the Second Amendment,* 9 HARV. J.L. & PUB. POL'Y 559, 562 (1986) (citing 1 JOHN J. BAGLEY & PETER B. ROWLEY, A DOCUMENTARY HISTORY OF ENGLAND 1066-1540, at 152 (1965)). This obligation continued for centuries, requiring nobility, and later commoners, to keep arms and participate in the militia. *Id.* at 563-65. The obligation to keep arms was not simply to provide military service in the king's army; English citizens were also required to provide local police services, such as pursuing criminals and guarding their villages. CLAYTON E. CRAMER, FOR THE DEFENSE OF THEMSELVES AND THE STATE: THE ORIGINAL INTENT AND JUDICIAL INTERPRETATION OF THE RIGHT TO KEEP AND BEAR ARMS 24-25 (1994); JOYCE LEE MALCOLM, TO KEEP AND BEAR ARMS: THE ORIGINS OF AN ANGLO-AMERICAN RIGHT 2 (1994).

By the middle of the seventeenth century, however, the sovereign jeopardized the individual right to bear arms. Charles II, and later James II, began to disarm many of their Protestant subjects. Hardy, *supra,* at 574-79. James II was an unpopular king whose policies stirred great resentment among both the political and religious communities of England. David E. Murley, *Private Enforcement of the Social Contract: Deshaney and the Second Amendment Right to Own Firearms,* 36 DUQ. L. REV. 15, 19 (1997). Eventually, James II fled England during what was later termed the Glorious Revolution. Hardy, *supra,* at 579. In the aftermath of the Glorious Revolution, Parliament passed the English Bill of Rights in 1689, codifying the individual right to bear arms. *Id.* at 580. The Bill of Rights provided that "the subjects which are Protestant may have arms for their defense suitable to their conditions and as allowed by law." *Id.* at 581.

b. *The Colonial Right To Bear Arms*

The American colonists exercised their right to bear arms under the English Bill of Rights. Indeed, the English government's success in luring Englishmen to America was due in part to pledges that the immigrants and their children would continue to possess "all the rights of natural subjects, as if born and abiding in England." MALCOLM, *supra,* at 138. As in England, the colonial militia played primarily a defensive role, with armies of volunteers organized whenever a campaign was necessary. *Id.* at 139. Statutes in effect bore evidence of an individual right to bear arms during colonial times. For example, a 1640 Virginia statute required "all masters of families" to furnish themselves and "all those of their families which shall be capable of arms . . . with arms both offensive and defensive." *Id.* (citing THE OLD DOMINION IN THE SEVENTEENTH CENTURY: A DOCUMENTARY HISTORY OF VIRGINIA, 1606-1689, at 172 (Warren M. Billings ed., 1975). A 1631 Virginia law required "all men that are fittinge to beare armes, shall bring their pieces to church . . . for drill and target practice." Hardy, *supra,* at 588 (quoting 1 WILLIAM W. HENING, THE STATUTES AT LARGE: BEING A COLLECTION OF ALL THE LAWS OF VIRGINIA FROM THE FIRST SESSION OF THE LEGISLATURE IN THE YEAR 1619, at 173-74 (reprint. 1969) (1823). These laws served the twofold purpose of providing individual self-defense while giving England a reserve force available in time of war. Murley, *supra,* at 20.

Following the French and Indian War, England increased taxes and stationed a large army in the colonies. On April 3, 1769, the *Boston Evening Post* announced that colonial authorities urged the citizenry to take up arms. In reply to the claim that this request was unlawful, the newspaper observed that:

> It is certainly beyond human art and sophistry, to prove the British subjects, to whom the *privilege* of possessing arms as expressly recognized by the Bill of Rights, and who live in a province where the law requires them to be equipped with *arms,* are guilty of an *illegal act,* in calling upon one another to be provided with them, as the *law directs*.

Hardy, *supra,* at 589-90 (quoting OLIVER M. DICKERSON, BOSTON UNDER MILITARY RULE 61 (1936)). Shortly after the "Boston Tea Party," British soldiers, led by General Gage, attempted to disarm the colonists. MALCOLM, *supra,* at 144. The British Parliament banned all exports of muskets and ammunition to the colonies and began seizing the colonists' weapons and ammunition. *Id.* The British efforts to disarm the colonists hardened American resistance. At that point, the colonists began to form the "minutemen," a nationwide select militia organization. Hardy, *supra* at 890. In February 1775, a colonial militia prevented the British from seizing weapons at an armory in Salem, Massachusetts. Two months later, the colonists defeated British troops at Concord. *Id.* at 591. Distinguished colonial leaders, such as George Washington and Samuel Adams, strongly influenced the organization of these local militias. STEPHEN P. HALBROOK, THAT EVERY MAN BE ARMED: THE EVOLUTION OF A CONSTITUTIONAL RIGHT 60-61 (1984).

The "militia" which won the Revolutionary War consisted of all who were treated as full citizens of the community. George Mason stated, "Who are the militia? They consist now of the whole people." Sanford Levinson, *The Embarrassing Second Amendment,* 99 Yale L.J. 637, 647 (1989) (citing statement of George Mason (June 14, 1788), *in* 3 JONATHAN ELLIOTT, DEBATES IN THE GENERAL STATE CONVENTIONS 425 (3d ed. 1937)). Similarly, the Federal Farmer referred to a "militia, when properly formed, [as] in fact the people themselves." *Id.* (quoting RICHARD HENRY LEE, OBSERVATIONS LEADING TO A FAIR EXAMINATION OF THE SYSTEM OF GOVERNMENT PROPOSED BY THE LATE CONVENTION: LETTERS FROM THE FEDERAL FARMER TO THE REPUBLICAN 123 (Walter H. Bennett ed., 1978)).

The individual right to bear arms, a right recognized in both England and the colonies, was a crucial factor in the colonists' victory over the British army in the Revolutionary War. Without that individual right, the colonists never could have won the Revolutionary War. After declaring independence from England and establishing a new government through the Constitution, the American founders sought to codify the individual right to bear arms, as did their forebears one hundred years earlier in the English Bill of Rights.

c. *The Ratification Debates*

A foundation of American political thought during the Revolutionary period was the well justified concern about political corruption and governmental tyranny. Even the federalists, fending off their opponents who accused them of creating an oppressive regime, were careful to acknowledge the risks of tyranny. Against that backdrop, the framers saw the personal right to bear arms as a potential check against tyranny. Theodore Sedgwick of Massachusetts expressed this sentiment by declaring that it is "a chimerical idea to suppose that a country like this could ever be enslaved . . . Is it possible . . . that an army could be raised for the purpose of enslaving themselves or their brethren? or, if raised whether they could subdue a nation of freemen, who know how to prize liberty and who have arms in their hands?" MALCOLM, *supra* at 157 (citing 2 JONATHAN ELLIOT, THE DEBATES IN THE SEVERAL STATE CONVENTIONS ON THE ADOPTION OF THE FEDERAL CONSTITUTION 97 (2d ed. 1863)). Noah Webster similarly argued:

> Before a standing army can rule the people must be disarmed; as they are in almost every kingdom in Europe. The supreme power in America cannot enforce unjust laws by the sword; because the whole body of the people are armed, and constitute a force superior to any band of regular troops that can be, on any pretence, raised in the United States.

Id. (citing NOAH WEBSTER, AN EXAMINATION INTO THE LEADING PRINCIPLES OF THE FEDERAL CONSTITUTION (1787), *reprinted in* PAMPHLETS ON THE CONSTITUTION OF THE UNITED STATES, PUBLISHED DURING ITS DISCUSSION BY THE PEOPLE, 1787-1788, at 56 (Paul L. Ford, ed. 1971) (1888)). Richard Lee Henry's view that a well regulated militia was the entire armed populace rather than a select body of men was reiterated by proponents to a bill of rights. As "M.T. Cicero" wrote to "The Citizens of America":

> Whenever, therefore, the profession of arms becomes a distinct order in the state . . . the end of the social compact is defeated . . . .
> No free government was ever founded, or ever preserved its liberty, without uniting the characters of the citizen and the soldier in those destined for the defence of the state . . . . Such are a well regulated militia, composed of the freeholders, citizen and husbandman, who take up arms to preserve their property, as individuals, and their rights as freemen. HALBROOK, *supra* at 72 (citing STATE GAZETTE (Charleston), Sept. 8, 1788).

George Mason argued the importance of the militia and right to bear arms by reminding his compatriots of England's efforts "to disarm the people; that it was the best and most effectual way to enslave them . . . by totally disusing and neglecting the militia." *Id.* at 74 (citing 3 JONATHAN ELLIOT, THE DEBATES IN THE SEVERAL STATE CONVENTIONS ON THE ADOPTION OF THE FEDERAL CONSTITUTION 380 (2d ed. 1863)). He also clarified that under prevailing practice the militia included all people, rich and poor. "Who are the militia? They consist now of the whole people, except a few public officers." *Id.* (citing 3 ELLIOT at 425-26). Because all were members of the militia, all enjoyed the right to individually bear arms to serve therein.

The framers thought the personal right to bear arms to be a paramount right by which other rights could be protected. Therefore, writing after the ratification of the Constitution, but before the election of the first Congress, James Monroe included "the right to keep and bear arms" in a list of basic "human rights" which he proposed to be added to the Constitution. HALBROOK, *supra* at 223 n. 145 (citing James Monroe Papers, New York Public Library (Miscellaneous Papers of James Monroe)).

The framers also saw an armed populace as the safeguard of religious liberty. Zachariah Johnson told the Virginia convention their liberties would be safe because

> the people are not to be disarmed of their weapons. They are left in full possession of them. The government is administered by the representatives of the people, voluntarily and freely chosen. Under these circumstances should anyone attempt to establish their own system [of religion], in prejudice of the rest, they would be universally detested and opposed, and easily frustrated. This is the principle which secures religious liberty most firmly. The government will depend on the assistance of the people in the day of distress.

MALCOLM, *supra* at 157 (citing 3 ELLIOT 646)).

Patrick Henry, also in the Virginia convention, eloquently argued for the dual rights to arms and resistance to oppression: "Guard with jealous attention the public liberty. Suspect everyone who approaches that jewel. Unfortunately, nothing will preserve it but downright force. Whenever you give up that force, you are ruined." HALBROOK, *supra* at 73 (citing 3 ELLIOT at 45). Thus, the federalists agreed with Blackstone that an armed populace was the ultimate check on tyranny. MALCOLM, *supra* at 157.

While both Monroe and Adams supported ratification of the Constitution, its most influential framer was James Madison. In The Federalist No. 46, he confidently contrasted the federal government of the United States to the European despotisms which he contemptuously described as "afraid to trust the people with arms." He assured his fellow citizens that they need never fear their government because of "the advantage of being armed." Don B. Kates, Jr., *Handgun Prohibition and The Original Meaning of The Second Amendment,* 82 MICH. L. REV. 204, 228 (1983) (quoting THE FEDERALIST NO. 46, at 371 (James Madison) (John. C. Hamilton ed., 1864)).

Many years later, Madison restated the sentiments of The Federalist No. 46 by declaring: "[A] government resting on a minority is an aristocracy, not a Republic, and could not be safe with a numerical and physical force against it, without a standing army, an enslaved press, and a disarmed populace." *Id.* (quoting RALPH L. KETCHAM, JAMES MADISON: A BIOGRAPHY 64, 640 (1971)).

Although on the other side of the ratification debate, Anti-Federalist Patrick Henry was unequivocal on the individual right to bear arms. During the Virginia ratification convention, he objected to the Constitution's inclusion of clauses specifically authorizing a standing army and giving the federal government control of the militia. He also objected to the omission of a clause forbidding disarmament of the individual citizen: "The great object is that every man be armed. . . . [e]veryone who is able may have a gun." *Id.* at 229 (citing 3 J. ELLIOTT, *supra,* at 45).

By January of 1788, Delaware, Pennsylvania, New Jersey, Georgia and Connecticut ratified the Constitution without insisting upon amendments. Several specific amendments were proposed, but were not adopted at the time the Constitution was ratified. The Pennsylvania convention, for example, debated fifteen amendments, one of which concerned the right of the people to be armed, another with the militia. The amendment on the right to bear arms read:

> That the people have a right to bear arms for the defence of themselves and their own State, or the United States, or for the purpose of killing game; and no law shall be passed for disarming the people or any of them, unless for crimes committed, or real danger of public injury from individuals; and as standing armies in time of peace are dangerous to liberty, they ought not to be kept up; and that the military shall be kept under strict subordination to and be governed by the civil power.

14

MALCOLM, *supra* at 158 (citing PENNSYLVANIA AND THE FEDERAL CONSTITUTION, 1787-1788, at 422).

The Massachusetts convention also ratified the Constitution with an attached list of proposed amendments. *Id.* In the end, the ratification convention was so evenly divided between those for and against the Constitution that the federalists agreed to amendments to assure ratification. *Id.* Samuel Adams proposed that the Constitution:

> [B]e never construed to authorize Congress to infringe the just liberty of the press, or the rights of conscience; or to prevent the people of the United States, who are peaceable citizens, from keeping their own arms; or to raise standing armies, unless when necessary for the defence of the United States, or of some one or more of them; or to prevent the people from petitioning, in a peaceable and orderly manner, the federal legislature, for a redress of their grievances: or to subject the people to unreasonable searches and seizures.

Id. (citing DEBATES AND PROCEEDINGS IN THE CONVENTION OF THE COMMONWEALTH OF MASSACHUSETTS, HELD IN THE YEAR 1788, at 198-99 (Bradford Pierce and Charles Hale, ed., 1856)).

Other states which had not yet ratified the Constitution followed the Maryland convention's practice of ratifying the Constitution while submitting proposed amendments. The New Hampshire convention, for example, adopted the nine Massachusetts amendments and added three others: one to limit standing armies, a second to ensure an individual right to bear arms, and a third to protect freedom of conscience. *Id.* The proposed amendment on freedom to bear arms read: "Congress shall never disarm any Citizen unless such as are or have been in Actual Rebellion." *Id.* at 158-59 (citing 2 DOCUMENTARY HISTORY OF THE CONSTITUTION OF THE UNITED STATES, 1787-

1870, at 143 (1894)).

d. Drafting the Second Amendment

When the first Congress convened on March 4, 1789, James Madison, who had previously advocated passage of the Constitution without amendments, now pressed his colleagues to act on a bill of rights. MALCOLM, *supra* at 159. When his initial efforts failed to produce any response, he drafted his own version of a bill of rights and presented them to members of Congress on June 8 of that year. *Id.* He explained to Jefferson that he deliberately drafted the amendments to be unexceptional and therefore likely to win approval. *Id.* (citing RONALD RUTLAND, THE BIRTH OF THE BILL OF RIGHTS 209 (1991)). His version of what would later be the second amendment read:

> The right of the people to keep and bear arms shall not be infringed; a well armed, and well regulated militia being the best security of a free country: but no person religiously scrupulous of bearing arms, shall be compelled to render military service in person.

MALCOLM, *supra* at 159.

That Madison envisioned a personal right to bear arms, rather than merely a right for the states to organize militias, is evident from his desired placement of the right in the Constitution. Madison's original plan was to designate the amendments as inserts between specific sections of the existing Constitution, rather than as separate amendments added to the end of the document. Hardy, *supra* at 609 (citing 1 ANNALS OF CONGRESS 707-08 (Joseph Gales ed., 1789)). Madison did not designate the right to keep and bear arms as a limitation of the militia clause of Section 8 of Article I. Rather, he placed it as part of a group of provisions (with freedom of speech and the press) to be inserted in "Article 1st, Section 9, between

16

Clauses 3 and 4." *Id.* (quoting 5 DOCUMENTARY HISTORY OF THE CONSTITUTION OF THE UNITED STATES OF AMERICA 186-87 (1905)). Such a designation would have placed this right immediately following the few individual rights protected in the original Constitution, dealing with the suspension of bills of attainder, habeas corpus, and ex post facto laws. Thus Madison aligned the right to bear arms along with the other individual rights of freedom of religion and the press, rather than with congressional power to regulate the militia. *Id.* This suggested placement of the Second Amendment reflected recognition of an individual right, rather than a right dependent upon the existence of the militia.

At that point, the Senate took up the Bill of Rights. Unfortunately, Senate debate on the issue was held in secret, and therefore no record exists of that body's deliberations. CRAMER, *supra* at 58 (citing HELEN VEIT ET AL., CREATING THE BILL OF RIGHTS: THE DOCUMENTARY RECORD FROM THE FIRST FEDERAL CONGRESS xix (1991)). The Senate form of the second amendment now described the militia not as "the best security" of a free state, but as "necessary to the security" of a free state, an even stronger endorsement than Madison's original description. MALCOLM, *supra* at 161. The Senators also omitted the phrase describing the militia as "composed of the body of the people." Elbridge Gerry's fear that future Congresses might expand on the religious exemption clause evidently convinced the Senate to eliminate that clause as well. *Id.* Even more important, however, was the Senate's refusal of a motion to add "for the common defense" after the phrase "to keep and bear arms." *Id.* (citing HALBROOK, *supra* at 81, n. 167). Thus the American Bill of Rights, like the English Bill of Rights, recognized the individual's right to have weapons for his own defense, rather than for collective defense. *Id.* In this form, Congress approved the Second Amendment and sent the Bill of Rights to the state legislatures for ratification. *Id.*

In retrospect, the framers designed the Second

Amendment to guarantee an individual's right to arms for self-defense. Such an individual right was the legacy of the English Bill of Rights. American colonial practice, the constitutional ratification debates, and state proposals over the amendment all bear this out. *Id.* at 162. The American Second Amendment also expanded upon the English Bill of Rights' protection; while English law allowed weapons "suitable to a person's condition" "as allowed by law," the American right forbade any "infringement" upon the right of the people to keep and bear arms. *Id.*

In his influential *Commentaries on the Constitution,* Joseph Story emphasized the importance of the Second Amendment. He described the militia as the "natural defence of a free country" not only "against sudden foreign invasions" and "domestic insurrections," but also against "domestic usurpations of power by rulers." He went on to state that "[t]he right of the citizens to keep and bear arms has justly been considered as the palladium of the liberties of a republic; since it offers a strong moral check against the usurpation and arbitrary power of rulers; and will generally, even if these are successful in the first instance, enable the people to resist and triumph over them." 3 J. Story, Commentaries § 1890, p. 746 (1833).

4. STRUCTURAL ANALYSIS

The structure of the Second Amendment within the Bill of Rights proves that the right to bear arms is an individual right, rather than a collective one. The collective rights' idea that the Second Amendment can only be viewed in terms of state or federal power "ignores the implication that might be drawn from the Second, Ninth, and Tenth Amendments: the citizenry itself can be viewed as an important third component of republican governance as far as it stands ready to defend republican liberty against the depredations of the other two structures, however futile that might appear as a practical matter." Sanford Levinson, *The Embarrassing Second Amendment,* 99 YALE L.J. 637, 651 (1989).

Furthermore, the very inclusion of the right to keep and bear arms in the Bill of Rights shows that the framers of the Constitution considered it an individual right. "After all, the Bill of Rights is not a bill of states' rights, but the bill of rights retained by the people." David Harmer, *Securing a Free State: Why The Second Amendment Matters,* 1998 BYU L. REV. 55, 60 (1998). Of the first ten amendments to the Constitution, only the Tenth concerns itself with the rights of the states, and refers to such rights in addition to, not instead of, individual rights. *Id.* Thus the structure of the Second Amendment, viewed in the context of the entire Bill of Rights, evinces an intent to recognize an individual right retained by the people.

5. JUDICIAL INTERUPERATIONS

The Court notes that several other federal courts have held that the Second Amendment does not establish an individual right to keep and bear arms, but rather a "collective" right, or a right held by the states. *See, e.g., Hickman v. Block,* 81 F.3d 98, 100-01 (9th Cir. 1996) (holding that plaintiff lacked standing to sue for denial of concealed weapons permit, because Second Amendment does not protect possession of weapon by private citizen; right to bear arms is held by the states); *Love v. Pepersack,* 47 F.3d 120, 124 (4th Cir. 1995) (holding that Second Amendment does not confer absolute individual right); *United States v. Warin,* 530 F.2d 103, 106-07 (6th Cir. 1976) (holding that Second Amendment guarantees a collective rather than an individual right; fact that an individual citizen, like all others, may enroll in state militia does not confer right to possess submachine gun); *Cases v. United States,* 131 F.2d 916, 920-23 (1st Cir. 1942) (holding that federal government may limit the keeping and bearing of arms by a single individual); *Hamilton v. Accu-Tek,* 935 F. Supp. 1307, 1318 (E.D.N.Y. 1996) (holding that Second Amendment right to bear arms establishes a collective rather than an individual or private right).

However, the only modern Second Amendment case from the Supreme Court is *United States v. Miller,* 307 U.S. 174 (1939). Jack Miller was charged with moving a sawed-off shotgun in interstate commerce in violation of the National Firearms Act of 1934. Among other things, Miller had not registered the firearm, as required by the Act. The court below dismissed the charge, accepting Miller's argument that the Act violated the Second Amendment.

The Supreme Court reversed unanimously, with Justice McReynolds writing the opinion. Interestingly enough, he emphasized that there was no evidence showing that a sawed-off shotgun "at this time has some reasonable relationship to the preservation or efficiency of a well regulated militia." *Id.* at 178. And "[c]ertainly it is not within judicial notice that this weapon is any part of the ordinary military equipment or that its use could contribute to the common defense." *Id.* at 178 (citation omitted). Thus, Miller might have had a tenable argument had he been able to show that he was keeping or bearing a weapon that clearly had a potential military use. Justice McReynolds went on to describe the purpose of the Second Amendment as "assur[ing] the continuation and render[ing] possible the effectiveness of [the Militia]." *Id.* at 178. He contrasted the Militia with troops of a standing army, which the Constitution indeed forbade the states to keep without the explicit consent of Congress. "The sentiment of the time strongly disfavored standing armies; the common view was that adequate defense of country and laws could be secured through the Militia—civilians primarily, soldiers on occasion." *Id.* at 179. McReynolds noted further that "the debates in the Convention, the history and legislation of Colonies and States, and the writings of approved commentators [all] [s]how plainly enough that the Militia comprised all males physically capable of acting in concert for the common defense." *Id.*

It is difficult to interpret *Miller* as rendering the Second Amendment meaningless as a control on Congress. Ironically, one can read *Miller* as supporting some of the most extreme anti-gun control arguments; for example, that the individual citizen has a right to keep and bear bazookas, rocket launchers, and other armaments that are clearly used for modern warfare, including, of course, assault weapons. Under *Miller,* arguments about the constitutional legitimacy of a prohibition by Congress of private ownership of handguns or, what is much more likely, assault rifles, thus might turn on the usefulness of such guns in military settings. Sanford Levinson, *The Embarrassing Second Amendment,* 99 YALE L.J. 637, 654-55 (1989).

Miller did not answer the crucial question of whether the Second Amendment embodies an individual or collective right to bear arms. Although its holding has been used to justify many previous lower federal court rulings circumscribing Second Amendment rights, the Court in *Miller* simply chose a very narrow way to rule on the issue of gun possession under the Second Amendment, and left for another day further questions of Second Amendment construction. *See Printz v. United States,* 521 U.S. 898, 937-38 & n.1, 2 (1997) (Thomas, J., concurring).

This Court has not had recent occasion to consider the nature of the substantive right safeguarded by the Second Amendment. [see footnote 2] If, however, the Second Amendment is read to confer a *personal* right to "keep and bear arms," a colorable argument exists that the Federal Government's regulatory scheme, at least as it pertains to the purely intrastate sale or possession of firearms, runs afoul of that Amendment's protections. [see footnote 3]

6. PRUDENTIAL CONCERNS

Some scholars have argued that even if the original intent of the Second Amendment was to provide an individual right to bear arms, modern-day prudential concerns about social costs outweigh such original intent and should govern current review of the amendment. However, there is a problem with such reasoning. If one accepts the plausibility of any of the arguments on behalf of a strong reading of the Second Amendment, but, nevertheless, rejects them in the name of social prudence and the present-day consequences of an individual right to bear arms, why do we not apply such consequentialist criteria to each and every part of the Bill of Rights? Levinson, *supra* at 658.

As Professor Ronald Dworkin has argued, what it means to take rights seriously is that one will honor them even when there is significant social cost in doing so. Protecting freedom of speech, the rights of criminal defendants, or any other part of the Bill of Rights has significant costs—criminals going free, oppressed groups having to hear viciously racist speech and so on—consequences which we take for granted in defending the Bill of Rights. This mind-set changes, however, when the Second Amendment is concerned. "Cost-benefit" analysis, rightly or wrongly, has become viewed as a "conservative" weapon to attack liberal rights. Yet the tables are strikingly turned when the Second Amendment comes into play. Here "conservatives" argue in effect that social costs are irrelevant and "liberals" argue for a notion of the "living Constitution" and "changed circumstances" that would have the practical consequence of erasing the Second Amendment from the Constitution. Levinson, *supra* at 657-58.

Other commentators, including Justice Scalia, have argued that even if there would be "few tears shed if and when the Second Amendment is held to guarantee nothing more than the state National Guard, this would simply show that the Founders were right when they feared that some future generation might wish to abandon liberties that they considered essential, and so sought to protect those liberties in a Bill of Rights. We may tolerate the abridgement of property rights and the elimination of a right to bear arms; but we should not pretend that these are not reductions of rights." Sanford Levinson, *Is the Second Amendment Finally Becoming Recognized As Part of the Constitution? Voices from the Courts,* 1998 BYU L. REV. 127, 132 (1998) (quoting Antonin Scalia,

Common-Law Courts in a Civil-Law System: The Role of United States Federal Courts in Interpreting the Constitution and Laws, in A Matter of Interpretation: Federal Courts and the Law 3, 43 (Amy Gutmann, ed. 1997).

In response to arguments propounded by Professor Laurence Tribe and others describing the Second Amendment as being simply "seemingly state-militia-based" rather than "supporting broad principles" of private ownership of guns, Justice Scalia pointed out that it is incorrect to assume that the word "militia" refers only to "'a select group of citizen-soldiers . . . rather than, as the Virginia Bill of Rights of June 1776 defined it, 'the body of the people, trained to arms.'" Antonin Scalia, Response, in *A Matter of Interpretation,* supra at 129, 136 n.13 (quoting JOYCE LEE MALCOLM, TO KEEP AND BEAR ARMS 136, 148 (1994)).

Justice Scalia also notes that "[t]his was also the conception of 'militia' entertained by James Madison," citing The Federalist No. 46 for support. *Id.* "It would also be strange," he goes on to say, "to find in the midst of a catalog of the rights of individuals a provision securing to the states the right to maintain a designated 'Militia.' Dispassionate scholarship suggests quite strongly that the right of the people to keep and bear arms meant just that." *Id.* at 137 n.13 (citing JOYCE LEE MALCOLM, TO KEEP AND BEAR ARMS (1994); William Van Alstyne, *The Second Amendment and the Personal Right to Arms,* 43 DUKE L.J. 1236 (1994)).

Justice Scalia concludes by stating that "[i]t is very likely that modern Americans no longer look contemptuously, as Madison did, upon the governments of Europe that 'are afraid to trust the people with arms,' The Federalist No. 46; and the . . . Constitution that Professor Tribe espouses will probably give effect to that new sentiment by effectively eliminating the Second Amendment. But there is no need to deceive ourselves as to what the original Second Amendment said and meant. Of course, properly understood, it is no limitation upon arms control by the states." *Id.*

Thus, concerns about the social costs of enforcing the Second Amendment must be outweighed by considering the lengths to which the federal courts have gone to uphold other rights in the Constitution. The rights of the Second Amendment should be as zealously guarded as the other individual liberties enshrined in the Bill of Rights.

7. CONSTITUTIONALITY OF 18 U.S.C. § 922(g)(8)

18 U.S.C. §922(g)(8) is unconstitutional because it allows a state court divorce proceeding, without particularized findings of the threat of future violence, to automatically deprive a citizen of his Second Amendment rights. The statute allows, but does not require, that the restraining order include a finding that the person under the order represents a credible threat to the physical safety of the intimate partner or child. 18 U.S.C. § 922(g)(8)(c)(i). If the statute only criminalized gun possession based upon court orders with particularized findings of the likelihood of violence, then the statute would not be so offensive, because there would be a reasonable nexus between gun possession and the threat of violence. However, the statute is infirm because it allows one to be subject to federal felony prosecution if the order merely "prohibits the use, attempted use, or threatened use of physical force against [an] intimate partner." 18 U.S.C. § 922(g)(8)(c)(ii).

However, prosecution based on such an order would be tautological, for § 922(g)(8)(c)(i) merely repeats in different wording the requirement in subsection (B) that the order "restrains such person from harassing, stalking, or threatening an intimate partner of such person or child of such intimate partner or person, or engaging in other conduct that would place an intimate partner in reasonable fear of bodily injury to the partner or child." §922 (g)(8)(B). All that is required for prosecution under the Act is a boilerplate order with no particularized findings. Thus, the statute has no real safeguards against an arbitrary abridgement of Second Amendment rights. Therefore, by criminalizing protected Second Amendment activity based upon a civil state court order with no particularized findings, the statute is over-broad and in direct violation of an individual's Second Amendment rights.

By contrast, §922(g)(8) is different from the felon-in-possession statute, 18 U.S.C. § 922(g)(1), because once an individual is convicted of a felony, he has by his criminal conduct taken himself outside the class of law-abiding citizens who enjoy full exercise of their civil rights. Furthermore, the convicted felon is admonished in state and federal courts that a felony conviction results in the loss of certain civil rights, including the right to bear arms. This is not so with § 922(g)(8). Under this statute, a person can lose his Second Amendment rights not because he has committed some wrong in the past, or because a judge finds he may commit some crime in the future, but merely because he is in a divorce proceeding. Although he may not be a criminal at all, he is stripped of his right to bear arms as much as a convicted felon. Second Amendment rights should not be so easily abridged.

It is absurd that a boilerplate state court divorce order can collaterally and automatically extinguish a law-abiding citizen's Second Amendment rights, particularly when neither the judge issuing the order, nor the parties nor their attorneys are aware of the federal criminal penalties arising from firearm possession after entry of the restraining order. That such a routine civil order has such extensive consequences totally attenuated from divorce proceedings makes the statute unconstitutional. There must be a limit to government regulation on lawful firearm possession. This statute exceeds that limit, and therefore it is unconstitutional.

C. Fifth Amendment

Emerson also contends that 18 U.S.C. § 922(g)(8) violates his Fifth Amendment due process rights. He argues that the perfunctory, generic temporary orders issued in his divorce proceedings expose him to federal criminal liability for engaging in otherwise lawful conduct.

Firearm possession is a valuable liberty interest imbedded in the Second Amendment to the United States Constitution. "[T]here is a long tradition of widespread lawful gun ownership by private individuals in this country." *Staples v. United States,* 511 U.S. 600, 610 (1994). Thus, Emerson has a protected liberty interest in firearm possession under the Fifth Amendment.

"It is wrong to convict a person of a crime if he had no reason to believe that the act for which he was convicted *was* a crime, or even that it was wrongful. This is one of the bedrock principles of American law. It lies at the heart of any civilized system of law." *United States v. Wilson,* 159 F.3d 280, 293 (7th Cir. 1998) (Posner, C.J., dissenting). It offends both substantive and procedural due process for Emerson to be convicted of a crime he did not know existed. Because 18 U.S.C. § 922(g)(8) is such an obscure criminal provision, it is unfair to hold him accountable for his otherwise lawful actions.

The conduct this statute criminalizes is *malum prohibitum,* not *malum in se.* In other words, there was nothing inherently evil about Emerson possessing a firearm while being under a domestic restraining order. His conduct was unlawful merely because the statute mandated that it be. *Wilson,* 159 F.3d at 294 (Posner, C.J., dissenting). Section 922(g)(8) is one of the most obscure of criminal provisions. Here, Emerson owned a firearm, and knew or should have known that if, for example, he was convicted of a felony, he would have to relinquish ownership of his firearm. If by chance he did not know this, the sentencing judge or the probation officer would have informed him of the law. Nevertheless, when Emerson was made subject to the restraining order telling him to not harass his wife, Emerson could not have known of the requirement to relinquish his gun unless the presiding judge issuing the order told him. In this case, the state district judge did not tell Emerson about the requirement. Emerson's attorney did not tell him either, because Emerson did not have a lawyer. The fact that the restraining order contained no reference to guns may have led Emerson to believe that since he complied with the order, he could carry on as before. *Id.* at 294-95.

Chief Judge Posner of the Seventh Circuit aptly explains the dilemma between the maxim "ignorance of the law is no excuse" and the inherent unreasonableness of criminal prosecutions involving obscure violations of law:

> We want people to familiarize themselves with the laws bearing on their activities. But a reasonable opportunity doesn't mean being able to go to a local law library and read Title 18. It would be preposterous to suppose that someone from [the defendant's] milieu is able to take advantage of such an opportunity. If none of the conditions that make it reasonable to dispense with proof of knowledge of the law is present, then to intone "ignorance of the law is no defense" is to condone a violation of fundamental principles for the sake of a modest economy in the administration of criminal justice.

Id. At 295.

Section 922(g)(8) is also one of those "highly technical statutes that present . . . the danger of ensnaring individuals engaged in apparently innocent conduct," of which the Supreme Court spoke in *Bryan v. United States,* 524 U.S. 184, 118 S. Ct. 1939, 1946-47, 141 L.Ed.2d 197 (1998). Emerson's case differs from *Bryan* because the statute in this case is easy to understand, but it is hard to discover, which in the end compels the same result as demonstrated by *Lambert v. California,* 355 U.S. 225 (1957).

In *Lambert,* a Los Angeles ordinance made it a crime for a convicted felon to remain in the city for more than five days without registering. Mrs. Lambert, a felon, failed to register. The Supreme Court held that the ordinance violated due process when applied to a person who had no notice of a duty to report. Id. at 229. The Court found that, while a legislative body may eliminate the *mens rea* from the elements of an offense, the constitutional requirement of due process of law places limits on this practice. Id. at 228. "[T]he existence of a *mens rea* is the rule of, rather than the exception to, the principles of Anglo-American criminal jurisprudence." *Staples,* 511 U.S. at 605 (citing *United States v. United States Gypsum Co.,* 438 U.S. 422, 436-37 (1978)). However, eliminating the *mens rea* requirement is such a fundamental departure from longstanding principles of criminal law that courts have demanded an indication of legislative intent to do so. *Staples,* 511 U.S. at 606. Due process requires some adequate, meaningful form of a fair warning or notice to a respondent to a protective order that he will be committing a crime if he possesses a firearm.

Because § 922(g)(8) is an obscure, highly technical statute with no *mens rea* requirement, it violates Emerson's Fifth Amendment due process rights to be subject to prosecution without proof of knowledge that he was violating the statute. Accordingly, Emerson's Motion to Dismiss the indictment as violative of the Fifth Amendment is granted.

D. Tenth Amendment

Emerson's last argument claims that 18 U.S.C. § 922(g)(8) violates the Tenth Amendment. The Tenth Amendment provides that:

> The powers not delegated to the United States by the Constitution, nor prohibited by it to the States, are reserved to the States respectively, or to the people.
> U.S. CONST. amend. X.

In *New York v. United States,* 505 U.S. 144 (1992), the Court noted that Tenth Amendment issues can be

resolved in one of two ways. The court can first in-
quire whether an Act of Congress is authorized by one
of the powers of Article I of the Constitution. Id. at
155 (citing, e.g., *Perez v. United States,* 402 U.S. 146
(1971); *McCulloch v. Maryland,* 4 Wheat 316 (1819)).
In other cases the court determines whether the Act of
Congress invades the province of state sovereignty
reserved by the Tenth Amendment. Id. (citing *Garcia
v. San Antonio Metro. Transit Auth.,* 469 U.S. 528
(1985); Lane County v. Oregon, 7 Wall. 71 (1869)).

"If a power is delegated to Congress in the Constitution, the Tenth Amendment expressly disclaims any
reservation of that power to the States; if a power is
an attribute of state sovereignty reserved by the
Tenth Amendment, it is necessarily a power the Constitution has not conferred on Congress." *New York,*
505 U.S. at 156 (citations omitted).

Because the Fifth Circuit has held that Congress
acted pursuant to its enumerated Commerce Clause
power under Article I, Congress therefore enacted 18
U.S.C. § 922 (g)(8) pursuant to a valid grant of power
in conformity with the Tenth Amendment. *United
States v. Pierson,* 139 F.3d 501 (5th Cir. 1998). As
mentioned previously, the court in *Pierson* held that
by creating a nexus between illegal firearm possession
and interstate commerce, Congress exercised its delegated power under the Commerce Clause to reach a
"discrete set of firearm possessions that additionally
have an explicit connection with or effect on interstate
commerce." *Id.* at 503. Therefore, under the first line
of inquiry set forth in *New York,* the statute is constitutional under the Tenth Amendment.

The Court now turns to the second line of inquiry,
whether the "Act of Congress invades the province of
state sovereignty reserved by the Tenth Amendment."
New York, 505 U.S. at 155. In *New York,* the Court
held that the Low-Level Radioactive Waste Policy
Amendments Act of 1985 unconstitutionally "com-
mandeer[ed] the legislative processes of the States by
directly compelling them to enact and enforce a federal regulatory program." *Id.* at 176 (quoting *Hodel v.
Virginia Surface Mining & Reclamation Ass'n, Inc.,*

452 U.S. 264, 288 (1981)).

In 1997, the Court refined this analysis by holding in *Printz v. United States* that Congress may act pursuant to its Commerce Clause powers and still violate principles of state sovereignty under the Tenth Amendment. 521 U.S. 898, 933 (1997). In *Printz,* the Brady Act commandeered state law enforcement officers to perform background checks on prospective handgun owners. The Court held unconstitutional this asserted power of the Federal Government "to impress into its service — and at no cost to itself — the police officers of the 50 states." *Id.* at 922.

By passing 18 U.S.C. § 922(g)(8), however, Congress did not violate the Tenth Amendment the way it did in *New York* and *Printz,* because here the federal government is not requiring state legislatures to pass specific laws, nor is it "commandeering" state governments into federal government service. Emerson argues, however, that § 922(g)(8) interferes with the ability of state judges to carry out their state's domestic relations laws, thus impermissibly regulating an area reserved for the states. It is true the Supreme Court has noted that family law is traditionally an area of state concern. *Hisquierdo v. Hisquierdo,* 439 U.S. 572,581(1979). And while it is arguable that § 922(g)(8) may offend general Tenth Amendment principles of federalism, because Congress was acting through an enumerated power in drafting the law, and the law does not command state activity in support of it, this statute does not clearly violate the Tenth Amendment under the Supreme Court's holdings in *New York* and *Printz.* Accordingly, Emerson's Tenth Amendment challenge to the statute fails.

III. CONCLUSION

Because 18 U.S.C. § 922(g)(8) violates the Second and Fifth Amendments to the United States Constitution, the Court GRANTS Emerson's Motion to Dismiss the Indictment. A judgment shall be entered in conformity with this opinion.

SO ORDERED.
Dated April 7, 1999

SAM R. CUMMINGS

UNITED STATES DISTRICT JUDGE

FOOTNOTES:

Footnote 1. On February 26, 1999, the Court granted Defendant's Motion to Dismiss. The following is the Court's memorandum opinion of the Order. Return to text of the Emerson Case.

Footnote 2. "Our most recent treatment of the Second Amendment occurred in *United States v. Miller,* 307 U.S. 174 (1939), in which we reversed the District Court's invalidation of the National Firearms Act, enacted in 1934. In *Miller,* we determined that the Second Amendment did not guarantee a citizen's right to possess a sawed-off shotgun because that weapon had not been shown to be 'ordinary military equipment' that could 'contribute to the common defense.' *Id.,* at 178. The Court did not, however, attempt to define, or otherwise construe, the substantive right protected by the Second Amendment." Return to text of the Emerson Case.

Footnote 3. "Marshaling an impressive array of historical evidence, a growing body of scholarly commentary indicates that the 'right to keep and bear arms' is, as the Amendment's text suggests, a personal right. See, *e.g.,* J. Malcolm, To Keep and Bear Arms: The Origins of an Anglo-American Right 162 (1994); S. Halbrook, That Every Man Be Armed, The Evolution of a Constitutional Right (1984);

GUN RIGHTS AFFIRMED

Van Alstyne, The Second Amendment and the Personal Right to Arms, 43 Duke L.J. 1236 (1994); Amar, The Bill of Rights and the Fourteenth Amendment, 101 Yale L.J. 1193 (1992); Control & Diamond, The Second Amendment: Toward an Afro-Americanist Reconsideration, 80 Geo. L.J. 309 (1991); Levinson, The Embarrassing Second Amendment, 99 Yale L.J. 637 (1989); Kates, Handgun Prohibition and the Original Meaning of the Second Amendment, 82 Mich. L. Rev. 204 (1983). Other scholars, however, argue that the Second Amendment does not secure a personal right to keep or bear arms. See, *e.g.,* Bogus, Race, Riots, and Guns, 66 S. Cal. L. Rev. 1365 (1993); Williams, Civic Republicanism and the Citizen Militia: The Terrifying Second Amendment, 101 Yale L.J. 551 (1991); Brown, Guns, Cowboys, Philadelphia Mayors, and Civic Republicanism: On Sanford Levinson's The Embarrassing Second Amendment, 99 Yale L.J. 661 (1989); Cress, An Armed Community: The Origins and Meaning of the Right to Bear Arms, 71 J. of Am. Hist. 22 (1984). Although somewhat overlooked in our jurisprudence, the Amendment has certainly engendered considerable academic, as well as public, debate."

 # Second Amendment Foundation

The following is a copy of the amicus curiae brief filed by the Second Amendment Foundation. In this brief, the Second Amendment Foundation points out to the Court that significant historical court cases as well as debates from the ratification of the United States Constitution defend the individual right to keep and bear arms.

The Second Amendment Foundation, hereinafter SAF, is a non-profit educational foundation dedicated to promoting a better understanding about our Constitutional heritage to privately own and possess firearms. SAF was incorporated in August 1974 under the laws of the State of Washington. It is a tax-exempt organization under §501 (c) (3) of the Internal Revenue Code. The Foundation's purpose is to preserve the effectiveness of the Second Amendment to the United States Constitution and provide aid and information to people throughout the United States. To that end, SAF carries on many nationally recognized educational and legal action programs designed to better inform the public about the gun control debate. SAF has a broad base of support with 600,000 members and supporters residing in every state of the union. In addition to numerous books, articles, and national seminars, SAF publishes the *Journal of Firearms and Public Policy*. A more detailed description of the SAF's work is found at its website (http://www.saf.org).

TABLE OF AUTHORITIES

Cases:

Houston v. Moore, 18 U.S. (5 Wheat.) 1 (1820)
Presser v. Illinois, 116 U.S. 252 (1886)
Scott v. Sandford, 60 U.S. 393 (1857)
State v. Newsom, 27 N.C. (5 Ired.) 203 (1844)
United States v. Cruikshank, 92 U.S. 542 (1875)
United States v. Emerson, 46 F. Supp. 2d 598 (N.D. Tex. 1999)
United States v. Miller, 307 U.S. 174 (1939)
United States v. Verdugo-Urquidez, 494 U.S. 259 (1990)

Constitutions and Statutes:

U.S. CONST. amend. II
U.S. CONST. art. I, Sec. 8
U.S. CONST. art. I, Sec. 9
U.S. CONST. art. III, Sec. 2
Penn. Const. (1776) *reprinted in* The Federal and State Constitutions, Colonial Charters, and Other Organic Laws of the States, Territories, and Colonies, Now or Heretofore Forming the United States of America 3082-3091 (Francis N. Thorpe, ed. 1909)
TEX. CONST. Art. I, § 23
WIS. CONST. Art. I, Sec. 25
18 U.S.C. § 922(g)(8)
A Bill for Preservation of Deer (Va., 1785) *reprinted in* 2 THE PAPERS OF THOMAS JEFFERSON 443 (J. Boyd ed. 1950-1982)
Enforcement Act of 1870, 16 Stat. 141 (1870)
7 The Statutes at Large, Being a Collection of all the Laws of Virginia, from the First Session of the Legislature, in the Year 1619 at 95 (W.W. Henning ed. 1823)

Law Reviews and Journals:

Don Kates, Handgun Prohibition and the Original Meaning of the Second Amendment, 82 MICH. L. REV. 204 (1983)
David B. Kopel, Clayton E. Cramer, and Scott G. Hattrup, *A Tale of Three Cities: The Right to Bear Arms in State Supreme Courts,* 68 TEMPLE L. REV. 1177(1995)

David B. Kopel, *The Second Amendment in the Nineteenth Century*, 1998 BYU L. REV. 1359, 1436-1441 (1998)

J. Neil Schulman, *The Text of the Second Amendment*, 4 J. FIREARMS & PUB. POL. 159 (1992)

Scott Bursor, Note, Toward a Functional Framework for Interpreting the Second Amendment, 74 TEX. L. REV. 1125 (1996)

Stefan B. Tahmassebi, *Gun Control and Racism*, GEO. MASON U. CIV. RTS. L. J. 61 (1991)

Stephen Halbrook, What the Framers Intended: A Linguistic Analysis of the Right to "Bear Arms", 49 LAW & CONTEMP. PROBS. 151 (1986)

Historical Documents: Debates, Letters, Resolutions and Newspaper Articles:

The Address and Reasons of Dissent of the Minority of the Convention of the State of Pennsylvania to their Constituents, PENNSYLVANIA PACKET (Philadelphia), December 18, 1787 reprinted in 2 THE DOCUMENTARY HISTORY OF THE RATIFICATION OF THE CONSTITUTION 618-639 (Merrill Jensen, John P. Kaminski, and Gaspare J. Saldino et al., eds. 1976)

House of Representatives, Debates, June 8, 1789, *reprinted in* 2 THE BILL OF RIGHTS: A DOCUMENTARY HISTORY 1016-1042 (Bernard Schwartz, ed. 1971)

House of Representatives, Proceedings on Amendments (July 28, 1789) *reprinted in* FREEMAN'S JOURNAL (Philadelphia), August 5, 1789, at 1

House of Representatives, Proceedings August 24, 1789 *reprinted in* 2 THE BILL OF RIGHTS: A DOCUMENTARY HISTORY 1138 (Bernard Schwartz, Ed. 1971)

JAMES MADISON, *Notes for Speech In Congress Supporting Amendments (June 8, 1789)*, in 12 THE PAPERS OF JAMES MADISON 193-195 (Robert A. Rutland and Charles F. Hobson, eds. 1979)

Letter from Frederick A. Muhlenberg (New York) to Benjamine Rush dated August 18, 1789 *in* CREATING THE BILL OF RIGHTS: THE DOCUMENTARY RECORD FOR THE FIRST FEDERAL CONGRESS 280-281 (Helen E. Veit, Kenneth R. Bowling, Charlene Bangs Bickford, eds.1991)

Letter from James Madison to Tench Coxe, June 24, 1789

in 12 THE PAPERS OF JAMES MADISON 258-259 (Robert A. Rutland and Charles F. Hobson, eds. 1979)

Letter from Joseph Jones (Richmond) to James Madison, June 24, 1789 *in* 12 THE PAPERS OF JAMES MADISON 258-259 (Robert A. Rutland and Charles F. Hobson, eds. 1979)

Letter from Thomas Jefferson to Justice William Johnson, June 12, 1823 *in* THE COMPLETE JEFFERSON 322 (Saul Padover, ed.)

Letter from William Grayson to Patrick Henry, June 12, 1789 *in* WILLIAM WIRT HENRY, 3 PATRICK HENRY: LIFE, CORRESPONDENCE AND SPEECHES, 391-392 (1891)

Letter from William L. Smith (New York) to Edward Rutledge, August 9, 1789 *in* CREATING THE BILL OF RIGHTS: THE DOCUMENTARY RECORD FOR THE FIRST FEDERAL CONGRESS 272-273 (Helen E. Veit, Kenneth R. Bowling, Charlene Bangs Bickford, eds.1991)

Letter to the Editors, Philadelphia Independent Gazetteer, August 20, 1789 *reprinted in* David E. Young, The Origin of the Second Amendment 701-702 (1995)

Proposed Declaration of Rights and other Amendments, Virginia Convention June 27, 1788 *reprinted in* 3 The Debates in the Several State Conventions, on the Adoption of the Federal Constitution, as recommended by the General Convention at Philadelphia in 1787 657-661 (Jonathan Elliot, ed. 1941)

Resolutions of New Hampshire, June 21, 1788 *reprinted in* THE DEBATES ON THE CONSTITUTION: PART 2 552 (1993)

Tench Coxe, *A Pennsylvanian,* Federal Gazette (Philadelphia), *reprinted in* David E. Young, The Origin of the Second Amendment: A Documentary History of the Bill of Rights 1787-1792 at 670-673 (1995)

2 The Bill of Rights: A Documentary History 681 (Bernard Schwartz, ed. 1971).

Other Sources:

David E. Young, The Origin of the Second Amendment: A Documentary History of the Bill of Rights 1787-1792 (1995)

Stephen Halbrook, That Every Man Be Armed: The Evolution of a Constitutional Right (1984)

Webster, An American Dictionary of the English Language (1828)

ARGUMENT AND AUTHORITIES

I. FACTS OF THE CASE

Dr. Timothy Joe Emerson is a 42-year-old Texas physician who operated a clinic in a poor area of San Angelo, Texas. His 29-year-old wife, Sasha, worked there as a nurse. In 1997, Dr. Emerson bought a Beretta pistol for self-defense after a drug addict threatened to kill everyone at the clinic.

Approximately one year later, Sasha filed for divorce and made a routine *ex parte* request for a temporary restraining order. The order, approved without a hearing, maintains the status quo by protecting the financial, property and parental rights of both parties. At a subsequent hearing, Dr. Emerson, representing himself, was called to testify by Mrs. Emerson's attorney regarding financial matters in order to determine temporary child support. The hearing included a brief colloquy between the judge and Mrs. Emerson. She noted that Dr. Emerson had never threatened her, though she said he had threatened her boyfriend. The judge found no evidence of any acts or threats of violence by Dr. Emerson against any member of his family.

When the temporary injunction was entered, Dr. Emerson was not informed that he could be subject to federal prosecution for possessing firearms while subject to this order. He was subsequently indicted for possession of a firearm, in violation of 18 U.S.C. § 922(g)(8). The federal District Court ruled that 18 U.S.C. § 922(g)(8) violated the Second and Fifth Amendments to the United States Constitution.[1]

II.   MADISON'S "NATURAL" "PRIVATE RIGHTS" AMENDMENT:

From Introduction to Passage by the House of Representatives Close examination of the development of the Second Amendment, from the day that

---

[1] *United States v. Emerson*, 46 F. Supp. 2d 598 (N.D. Tex. 1999).

Madison proposed it, through its passage by the U.S. House of Representatives, shows that the Amendment was universally considered to guarantee a private, personal right to possess firearms.[2]

A. Placement and selection of private rights

When James Madison introduced the right to keep and bear arms amendment, along with other proposed amendments, in Congress, he explained that these amendments protected what he described as "natural rights."[3] Because natural rights, by definition, are inherent human rights, natural rights cannot belong to governments (which do not exist in a state of nature), or to collective organizations (such as militias) which are part of organized society. Rights, such as Madison's Second Amendment right, which are "natural" must necessarily belong only to individuals.

Since Madison grouped his amendment proposals to be inserted within the Constitution next to related material, we can determine whether Madison understood his original draft of the Second Amendment as an "individual right" by examining where he placed it in relation to his other proposed individual rights protections, such as those found in the First, Third, Fourth, Fifth, Sixth, and Eighth Amendments.[4] Madison's Second Amendment related provision was positioned among his other "*natural*" or "*private rights*" proposals between the right to petition and that protecting against quartering of soldiers.

---

[2] While the amicus brief of Academics for the Second Amendment provides an excellent description of the Second Amendment's ratification, the Second Amendment Foundation brief looks more closely at a particular period in the ratification process.

[3] Madison's notes for his speech read, in part: "natural rights, retained - as Speech". JAMES MADISON, *Notes for Speech In Congress Supporting Amendments (June 8, 1789), in* 12 THE PAPERS OF JAMES MADISON 193-195 (Robert A. Rutland and Charles F. Hobson, eds. 1979) (hereinafter *Rutland*).

[4] House of Representatives, Debates (June 8, 1789) *reprinted in* 2 THE BILL OF RIGHTS: A DOCUMENTARY HISTORY 1016-1042 (Bernard Schwartz, ed. 1971) (source hereinafter *Schwartz*).

This placement of *the people's* right to keep and bear arms immediately after *the people's* right of petition and directly before protection against quartering soldiers remained the same in every Congressional listing of proposed amendments to the Constitution, including the Select Committee of Eleven proposals, the Committee of the Whole House proposals, the proposals of the House of Representatives, those of the Senate, those of the Conference Committee, and thus is in that same position today as part of the U.S. Bill of Rights. [5]

This consistent placement of *"the right of the people to keep and bear arms"* among other fundamental private rights belonging to *"the people"* is clear proof that Madison considered his proposal guaranteeing the right of the people to keep and bear arms and affirming the importance of the well regulated militia as protecting an individual right - like the right of individuals to speak, write, publish their sentiments, or petition government.

Madison distinguished "natural rights – retained" from "positive rights resulting – as trial by jury."[6] The distinction shows how selective Madison was regarding rights which we understand today as individual civil rights, but which Madison did not include in his collection of "private rights" because they also related to the judicial structure of the government. For example, Madison proposed to insert his amendment relating to the Seventh Amendment, jury trials in civil cases, in Article 3, Section 2, rather than include it in his private rights list. He did the same for the provisions for grand jury indictment and juries of the vicinage, which ultimately ended up as part of the Fifth and Sixth Amendments, respectively.[7] The proposed placement indicates that Madison considered the jury amendments as relating as more to the judicial system than to individual rights; that is why Madison

---

[5] House of Representatives, Proceedings on Amendments (July 28, 1789) *reprinted in* FREEMAN'S JOURNAL (Philadelphia), August 5, 1789, at 1.

[6] Rutland, supra note 3.

[7] Schwartz, supra note 4.

proposed to insert the jury amendments in Constitutional Articles dealing with the judicial branch of government, rather than where his list of natural or private rights would be inserted (in Article I, section 9). In Madison's view, the jury amendments did not relate solely to individual, natural or private rights the way all the other rights included in the "private rights" list did.

Madison did not propose any amendments to reduce the powers given to the Federal Government in Article 1, Section 8 of the Constitution. Section 8 grants Congress power to "provide for organizing, arming, and disciplining, the Militia..."[8]. If Madison believed the right to keep and bear arms amendment was principally about restricting federal militia powers, then Madison would have proposed inserting appropriate language in Article 1, Section 8. However, he did not make such a proposal.

By placing the right to arms amendment in Section 9, which already contained private rights, such as habeas corpus, Madison showed that the Second Amendment was primarily about "private rights." The language of the Second Amendment, as adopted, is consistent with Madison's "private rights" understanding. As Stephen Halbrook points out:

> If the framers had meant only to guarantee the right of states to have militias and of their organized militiamen to keep and bear arms, they would surely have worded the Second Amendment differently. Language such as "the right of the select militia to keep and bear arms" would have sufficed. It is unlikely that the framers would have intended to commit blatantly the fallacy of equivocation by shifting the meaning of "the people" from amendment to amendment, or that they would have risked the fallacy of ambiguity by defining the phrase "the people" in the Second Amendment in such an unusual manner, that is, as "those people in a select state militia." Such a bizarre inter-

---

[8] U.S. CONST. art. 1, Sec. 8.

pretation would also commit the fallacies of division and of composition in reverse by holding that the right exists in the whole but not in its parts or that it fails to exist in the parts but does exist in the whole.[9]

The Supreme Court has recognized the obvious import of the consistent use of language by Madison and the other framers. As the Court has pointed out, the phrase "the people," wherever it appears in the Constitution, has the same meaning, whether it be in the Second Amendment or in the Preamble to the Constitution or in the First, Fourth, Fifth, and Ninth Amendments.[10]

B. Commentary from the period supports private rights.

Not only did Madison himself view his Second Amendment proposal as relating only to private rights, but every comment from the period on Madison's proposals indicates that all the persons making the comments understood Madison's Second Amendment proposition the same way that Madison himself did - as involving only natural, personal, private, individual rights.

For example, on June 12, 1789, U.S. Senator William Grayson of Virginia wrote to Patrick Henry (who had introduced Virginia's proposed Bill of Rights and twenty other structural amendments to the Constitution into that state's Ratifying Convention) stating:

> Some gentlemen here from motives of policy have it in contemplation to effect amendments which shall effect personal liberty alone and further ..... Last Monday a string of amendments were presented to the lower

---

[9] Stephen Halbrook, That Every Man Be Armed: The Evolution of a Constitutional Right 85 (1984).

[10] United States v. Verdugo-Urquidez, 494 U.S. 259, 265 (1990).

House; these altogether respected personal
liberty. [11]

Senator Grayson referred to James Madison and
to Madison's proposed amendments, and he clearly
understood Madison's Bill of Rights proposals as relating to individual rights only. The reason for the
emphasis on personal liberty *alone* in Grayson's letter
is that the Virginia Anti-federalists, besides wanting
guarantees of private rights (such as the right to keep
and bear arms), also wanted a large number of other
amendments to reduce the powers which the main
body of the constitution had granted to the federal
government (such as federal militia powers). But
these hoped-for other amendments were not among
the complete set of amendments offered by Federalist
Madison.[12]

Madison acceded to the Virginia Ratifying Convention's demand for protection of the right of the
people to keep and bear arms, and he also offered language recognizing the importance of a well regulated
militia. But what Madison clearly chose not to do was
include the proposition protecting state power to provide for organizing, arming, and disciplining the militia, or any other change in the powers previously belonging only to the states and now given to the new
Federal Government, among any of his amendment
propositions. The state authority to provide for organizing, arming, and disciplining the militia provision
would have been directly contrary to every action the
Federalists had taken to create the Constitution,
which contained a list of powers for the new Federal
Government all of which were taken from, and were
stated to be paramount to the powers of, the state

---

[11] Letter from William Grayson to Patrick Henry, June 12, 1789 *in*
WILLIAM WIRT HENRY, 3 PATRICK HENRY: LIFE, CORRESPONDENCE AND
SPEECHES, 391-392 (1891).

[12] Proposed Declaration of Rights and other Amendments, Virginia Convention June 27, 1788 *reprinted in* 3 The Debates in the Several State
Conventions, on the Adoption of the Federal Constitution, as recommended by the General Convention at Philadelphia in 1787 657-661 (Jonathan Elliot, ed. 1941).

2nd Amendment Foundation Amicus Curiae

governments. Consequently, Article I, section 8, of the Constitution grants to Congress, rather than to the states, the power to "provide for organizing, arming, and disciplining, the Militia.[13]

On June 18, 1789, an article by the widely-read Federalist writer Tench Coxe appeared in a Philadelphia newspaper and was soon reprinted elsewhere, including New York. Coxe's two-part article described and explained each of Madison's proposed amendments to the Constitution. Coxe's description of the Second Amendment proposition was:

> As civil rulers, not having their duty to the people, duly before them, may attempt to tyrannize, and as the military forces which shall be occasionally raised to defend our country, might pervert their power to the injury of their fellow-citizens, the people are confirmed by the next article in their right to keep and bear their private arms.[14]

---

[13] Years later, during Madison's Presidency, the Supreme Court heard a case involving the boundaries between federal militia powers, and the states' authority over the militia. If the Second Amendment were in accord with the meaning given it by the Yassky brief, the Center to Prevent Handgun Violence, and the other gun prohibition amici, then the Second Amendment would have been the center of the Court's decision and of the parties' arguments. But in fact, neither party even mentioned the Second Amendment in argument, and the Court's decision was based on completely different grounds. *Houston v. Moore*, 18 U.S. (5 Wheat.) 1 (1820). For more detail on the *Houston* case, see David B. Kopel, *The Second Amendment in the Nineteenth Century*, 1998 BYU L. REV. 1359, 1381-87 (1998). Authors of nineteenth century constitutional treatises (such as Justice Story, William Rawle, and many others) who analyzed the boundaries of federal/state militia powers never suggested that the Second Amendment was even relevant to the issue. *Id.*

[14] Tench Coxe, *A Pennsylvanian*, FEDERAL GAZETTE (Philadelphia), *reprinted in* DAVID E. YOUNG, THE ORIGIN OF THE SECOND AMENDMENT: A DOCUMENTARY HISTORY OF THE BILL OF RIGHTS 1787-1792 at 670-673 (1995) (hereinafter *Origin of the Second Amendment*). Because Madison originally proposed more amendments than were eventually ratified, today's "Second Amendment" was not the second item on Madison's list. For convenience and consistency, this brief always uses "Second Amendment"— even though the Amendment was not second at all times.

Coxe sent a copy of the newspaper containing this article to James Madison and indicated that he was the author. Madison replied to Coxe indicating that Madison's amendments project "is therefore already indebted to the co-operation of your pen."[15]

Presumably, Madison would have corrected Coxe if Coxe had completely misinterpreted the Second Amendment, which would certainly have been the case if the exclusively collective right interpretation had any validity. However, Madison did not.

Likewise, On June 24, 1789, Joseph Jones, a member of the Virginia Council of State, wrote a letter to James Madison in which he stated:

> I thank you for a copy of the amendments proposed to the constitution which you lately inclosed to me - they are calculated to secure the personal rights of the people so far as declarations on paper can effect the purpose.[16]

Jones was clearly of the impression that Madison's list of "private rights" proposals related to "personal" or individual rights.

As the amendments worked their way through the House of Representatives, comments regarding them appeared in letters of members of Congress and in some newspaper articles. All of these, without exception, indicate that the Second Amendment and related amendments were universally understood to relate to private rights and personal liberty. For example, on August 9, 1789, U.S. Representative William L. Smith (South Carolina) wrote to Edward Rutledge:

> The Committee on amendmts. have reported some, which are thought inoffensive to the federalists . . . There appears to be a disposition in our house to agree to some, which will

---

[15] Letter from James Madison to Tench Coxe, June 24, 1789, *Rutland* at 258-259.

[16] Letter from Joseph Jones (Richmond) to James Madison (June 24, 1789), *Rutland* Vol. XII at 258-259.

more effectually secure private rights, without affecting the structure of Govt.[17]

The Federalists, the creators of the Constitution, were in control of Congress, and were not going to surrender any of the politically hard-won expansions of the federal government's powers, which had been achieved by the ratification of the Constitution. The Bill of Rights contained assurances about matters that the Federalists thought were beyond federal power even under the new Constitution; the Bill of Rights did not retract any of the federal powers which the Federalists had won just a few months before.

C. The Pennsylvania Minority

Speaker of the House, Frederick Augustus Muhlenberg, a leading Federalist from Pennsylvania, wrote on August 18th to Benjamin Rush in Philadelphia:

> But this Day has at length terminated the Subject of Amendments in the Committee of the whole House, & tomorrow we shall take up the Report & probably agree to the Amendments proposed, & which are nearly the same as the special Committee of eleven had reported them . . . I hope it will be satisfactory to our State, and as it takes in the principle Amendments which our Minority had so much at Heart.[18]

Three major points regarding the Speaker of the House's comments above are worthy of note:
First, the final amendments were considered to be

---

[17] Letter from William L. Smith (New York) to Edward Rutledge, August 9, 1789 *in* CREATING THE BILL OF RIGHTS: THE DOCUMENTARY RECORD FOR THE FIRST FEDERAL CONGRESS 272-273 (Helen E. Veit, Kenneth R. Bowling, Charlene Bangs Bickford, eds.1991) (hereinafter *Veit*).

[18] Letter from Frederick A. Muhlenberg (New York) to Benjamine Rush dated August 18, 1789, *Veit* at 280-281.

practically the same as the Committee of Eleven's proposals.[19]

Second, the Minority referred to by Speaker Muhlenberg was the Minority of the Pennsylvania Ratifying Convention. The Pennsylvania Minority had proposed amendments to the Constitution for protection of individual rights found today in the First, Second, Fourth, Fifth, Sixth, Seventh, and Eighth Amendments to the U.S. Constitution.[20] Pennsylvania's was the first state ratifying convention to meet after writing of the Constitution. The Pennsylvania Minority's arms rights provision was thus a

---

[19] An examination of the proposals from the Committee of Eleven (the Congressional committee that drafted the Bill of Rights) confirms that the Pennsylvania Speaker was plainly correct. House of Representatives, Proceedings on Amendments (July 28, 1789) *reprinted in* FREEMAN'S JOURNAL (Philadelphia), August 5, 1789, at 1 (hereinafter *House Proceedings*). Furthermore, the proposals of the House were practically the same as Madison's original propositions. House of Representatives, Debates (June 8, 1789), *Schwartz* at 1016-42.

Here are the House proposals relating to the Second Amendment in chronological order:

June 8, 1789. Madison's proposal:

The right of the people to keep and bear arms shall not be infringed; a well armed and well regulated militia being the best security of a free country; but no person religiously scrupulous of bearing arms shall be compelled to render military service in person.

Id.

July 28, 1789. Committee of Eleven's proposal:

A well regulated militia, composed of the body of the people, being the best security of a free state, the right of the people to keep and bear arms shall not be infringed, but no person religiously scrupulous shall be compelled to bear arms.

House Proceedings, supra.

August 24, 1789. House of Representatives' proposal:

Art. 5. A well regulated militia, composed of the body of the people, being the best security of a free state, the right of the people to keep and bear arms, shall not be infringed, but no one religiously scrupulous of bearing arms, shall be compelled to render military service in person.

House of Representatives Proceedings August 24, 1789, *Schwartz* at 1138.

[20] The Address and Reasons of Dissent of the Minority of the Convention of the State of Pennsylvania to their Constituents, PENNSYLVANIA PACKET (Philadelphia), December 18, 1787 reprinted in 2 THE DOCUMENTARY HISTORY OF THE RATIFICATION OF THE CONSTITUTION 618-639 (Merrill Jensen, John P. Kaminski, and Gaspare J. Saldino et al., eds. 1976) (hereinafter Pennsylvania Minority)

provision which Speaker Muhlenberg understood as relating to the U.S. House of Representatives proposed amendments. The Pennsylvania Minority had demanded a federal constitutional guarantee:

> 7. That the people have a right to bear arms for the defense of themselves and their own state, or the United States, or for the purpose of killing game; and no law shall be passed for disarming the people or any of them, unless for crimes committed, or real danger of public injury from individuals; and as standing armies in the time of peace are dangerous to liberty, they ought not to be kept up; and that the military shall be kept under strict subordination to and be governed by the civil power.[21]

This is an obvious early predecessor of the Second Amendment. The Pennsylvania Minority was doubtless inspired partly by the 1776 Pennsylvania State Declaration of Rights, which declared "That the people have a right to bear arms for the defence of *themselves* and the state."[22]

The third item worthy of note is what is entirely missing from the U.S. House of Representatives' amendments: a response to the Pennsylvania Minority's separate proposal for an amendment "that the power of organizing, arming, and disciplining the militia . . . remain with the individual states."[23]

Like the majority at the Virginia Ratifying Convention, the Minority at the Pennsylvania Ratifying Convention had put the hoped-for protection of state militia powers in a separate proposal from the hoped-for protection of the people's right to keep and bear

---

[21] Id.

[22] Penn. Const. (1776) *reprinted in* The Federal and State Constitutions, Colonial Charters, and Other Organic Laws of the States, Territories, and Colonies, Now or Heretofore Forming the United States of America 3082-3091 (Francis N. Thorpe, ed. 1909)

[23] Pennsylvania Minority, supra note 21.

arms. The Pennsylvanians and Virginians who advocated for constitutional amendments knew how to say in plain English that state governments should have more power over the militia. In all thirteen states, the people were not so incompetent at the English language that the phrase "the right of the people to keep and bear arms" would be used when what was actually meant was "the power of state governments to organize, arm, and discipline the militia."

B. Samuel Adams' Proposal at the Massachusetts Convention

On August 20, 1789 the Philadelphia Independent Gazetteer published an article relating to the amendments in Congress which included the statement:

every one of the intended alterations, but one, have been already reported by the committee of the House of Representatives in Congress[24]

The *"intended alterations"* referred to were the failed proposal for a short bill of rights by Samuel Adams in the Massachusetts Ratifying Convention. Here is what Samuel Adams had proposed on February 6, 1788:

And that the said Constitution be never construed to authorize Congress to infringe the just liberty of the press, or the rights of conscience; or to prevent the people of the United States, who are peaceable citizens, from keeping their own arms; or to raise standing armies, unless when necessary for the defense of the United States, or of some one or more of them; or to prevent the people from petitioning, in a peaceable and orderly manner, the federal legislature, for a re-

---

[24] Letter to the Editors, PHILADELPHIA INDEPENDENT GAZETTEER, August 20, 1789 *reprinted in The Origin of the Second Amendment* at 701-702. For the convenience of the Court and the parties, the Second Amendment Foundation has donated a copy of *The Origin of the Second Amendment* to each party, several copies to the Fifth Circuit Library as well as a relevant letter from David Young. *The Origin* is the only comprehensive collection of original documents regarding the Second Amendment from 1787 to 1792. *See* http://www.saf.org/Young.html

dress of grievances; or to subject the people to unreasonable searches and seizures of their persons, papers or possessions.[25]

All of Adams' "intended alterations, but one" had been passed by the U.S. House of Representatives. The "but one" is obviously Adams' call for limits on Congressional power to raise standing armies–since the U.S. House never passed such a proposed alteration. Therefore, because all "but one" of Adams' proposals had been adopted by the U.S. House, the U.S. House must have adopted Adams proposal that Congressional powers never be construed "to prevent the people of the United States, who are peaceable citizens, from keeping their own arms."

James Madison proposed that the U.S. House of Representatives adopt an amendment to protect the "private rights" of the people to keep and bear arms, and the House did so. The newspaper record and records of the Founders' correspondence show that the American people understood the Second Amendment to protect a personal right to arms–and not a restriction on federal militia powers.

III. THE TEXT OF THE SECOND AMENDMENT

Part II of this brief showed that the Second Amendment was intended and understood to guarantee a "private right." Part III of this brief shows how the Amendment's text carries out that intent.

The Second Amendment states that:

> A well regulated Militia, being necessary to the security of a free State, the right of the people to keep and bear Arms, shall not be infringed.

The words "A well-regulated militia, being necessary to the security of a free state" constitutes a pre-

---

[25] 2 The Bill of Rights: A Documentary History 681 (Bernard Schwartz, ed. 1971).

sent participle. "Being necessary to the security of a free State" is an adjectival phrase, modifying "militia," which is followed by the main clause of the sentence (subject "right," verb "shall").

Grammatically speaking, "being necessary to the security of a free state", does not restrict the right to keep and bear arms, nor is the language "the right of the people to keep and bear arms" conditioned by a "well-regulated militia."[26] The main (independent) clause of the Second Amendment makes a positive statement with respect an unconditional, inherent individual right.[27]

According to Webster's, to *"bear"* *"arms"* simply means *"carrying"* or *"wearing"* weapons on the person or inside one's clothing.[28] Webster's definition of "arms," does not imply an exclusively military usage: "Weapons of offense, or armor for defense and protection of the body." [29]

> Furthermore,
> That to "bear" arms means simply to carry them was clear in a game bill drafted by Thomas Jefferson and proposed by James Madison, draftsman of the second amendment, in the Virginia legislature. The bill would have fined those who hunted deer out of season, and if within a year "[the hunter] shall bear a gun out of his inclosed ground, unless whilst performing military duty," he shall be in violation of his recognizance. The game violator would have to go back to court for "every such bearing of a gun" to be again

---

[26] *See* J. Neil Schulman, *The Text of the Second Amendment*, 4 J. FIREARMS & PUB. POL. 159 (1992) http://www.saf.org/journal/4_Schulman.html

[27] *See,* Stephen Halbrook, That Every Man Be Armed: The Evolution of a Constitutional Right 84 (1984).

[28] Webster, An American Dictionary of the English Language (1828).

[29] For a word-by-word analysis of Webster's Dictionary applied to the Second Amendment, see David B. Kopel, *The Second Amendment in the Nineteenth Century*, 1998 BYU L. REV. 1359, 1404-09 (1998).

bound to his good behavior. Thus, in the minds of Thomas Jefferson and James Madison, to "bear" a gun meant to carry it about in one's hands or on one's person, as for instance a deer hunter would do. "Bearing arms" is not associated with militia duty only, for the language above addresses the "bearing of a gun" by any person when not "performing military duty."[30]

The claim that the term *the people* in the Second Amendment refers only to state governments rather than individuals is inconsistent with other provisions of the Bill of Rights and its history as discussed above. As constitutional scholar Don Kates points out:

> The second amendment's literal language creates another, even more embarrassing problem for the exclusively state's right interpretation. To accept such an interpretation requires the anomalous assumption that the Framers ill-advisedly used the phrase "right of the people" to describe what was being guaranteed when what they actually meant was "right of the states." In turn, that assumption leads to a host of further anomalies. The phrase "the people" appears in four other provisions of the Bill of Rights, always denoting rights pertaining to individuals. Thus, to justify an exclusively state's right view, the following set of propositions must be accepted: (1) when the first Congress drafted the Bill of Rights it used "right of the people" in the first amendment to denote a right of individuals (assembly); (2) then, some sixteen

---

[30] Stephen Halbrook, *What the Framers Intended: A Linguistic Analysis of the Right to "Bear Arms"*, 49 LAW & CONTEMP. PROBS. 151 at 153-156 (1986), *citing* A Bill for Preservation of Deer (Virginia, 1785) *reprinted in* 2 THE PAPERS OF THOMAS JEFFERSON 443 (J. Boyd ed. 1950-1982).

words later, it used the same phrase in the
second amendment to denote a right belonging exclusively to the states; (3) but then,
forty-six words later, the fourth amendment's
"right of the people" had reverted to its normal individual right meaning; (4) "right of the
people" was again used in the natural sense
in the ninth amendment; and (5) finally, in
the tenth amendment the first Congress specifically distinguished "the states" from "the
people," although it had failed to do so in the
second amendment. Any one of these textual
incongruities demanded by an exclusively
state's right position dooms it. Cumulatively
they present a truly grotesque reading of the
Bill of Rights. [31]

This textual analysis is supported by the ratifica-
tions and resolutions of the seven state conventions
held in 1788.[32] This is especially relevant here because:

Madison drafted the Bill of Rights with the
aid of innumerable suggestions from his
countrymen, most commonly in the form of
the state bills of rights and the hundreds of
amendments suggested by the state conventions that ratified the Constitution. Indeed,
Madison began his work by purchasing a
pamphlet that listed over two hundred demands of the state conventions, eliminating

---

[31] Don Kates, Handgun Prohibition and the Original Meaning of the Second Amendment, 82 MICH. L. REV. 204, 219 (1983).

[32] As Thomas Jefferson advised:
On every question of construction [of the Constitution] let us carry ourselves back to the time when the Constitution was adopted, recollect the
spirit manifested in the debates, and instead of trying what meaning may
be squeezed out of the text, or invented against it, conform to the probable
one in which it was passed.
Letter from Thomas Jefferson to Justice William Johnson, June 12, 1823
in THE COMPLETE JEFFERSON 322 (Saul Padover, ed.).

some, and rewording and consolidating as many as possible to develop the Bill of Rights. Drafted with an eye toward earning the approval of the statehouses, the Bill of Rights was thus infused from the bottom up with the dominant ideology of the day.[33]

The common theme running through these state conventions which took place in the spring and summer of 1788 was the clear and unequivocal understanding that the right to keep and bear arms belonged to "the people" independent of "the state". For example, in the New Hampshire convention held on June 21, 1788, the delegates adopted the following language:

Congress shall never disarm any citizen, unless such as are or have been in actual rebellion.[34]

These provisions recollect the spirit at the time when the Constitution was adopted which was the simple recognition that "the people" have liberty to keep and bear arms to fulfill various individual needs, including self-defense.[35]

IV.   SUPREME COURT INTERPRETATIONS FROM THE 19TH CENTURY SHOW THAT THE COURT UNDERSTOOD THE

---

[33] Scott Bursor, Note, Toward a Functional Framework for Interpreting the Second Amendment, 74 TEX. L. REV. 1125, 1130 (1996).

[34] Resolutions of New Hampshire, June 21, 1788, *reprinted in* THE DEBATES ON THE CONSTITUTION: PART 2 552 (1993)

[35] The inherent right to keep and bear arms for various individual needs is now recognized in one form or another by the constitutions of 44 states. *See,* David B. Kopel, Clayton E. Cramer, and Scott G. Hattrup, *A Tale of Three Cities: The Right to Bear Arms in State Supreme Courts*, 68 TEMPLE L. REV. 1177, 1180 (1995) (n.13).
For example, TEX. CONST. Art. I, § 23 states:
Every citizen shall have the right to keep and bear arms in the lawful defense of himself or the State; but the Legislature shall have power, by law, to regulate the wearing of arms, with a view to prevent crime.

The Wisconsin provision, added by the voters in 1998, states:
The people have the right to keep and bear arms for security, defense, hunting, recreation or any other lawful purpose.
WIS. CONST. Art. I, § 25.

SECOND AMENDMENT TO BE A
PRIVATE RIGHT

The Supreme Court has rarely directly-addressed the Second Amendment. The last occasion was over fifty years ago in 1939.[36] While the *Miller* case has already been addressed by the parties and other *amicus curiae*, SAF will examine some of the Supreme Court's earlier rulings to show that the Court has understood and specifically recognized the Second Amendment as a private, individual right belonging to all citizens of the United States.

A. *Dred Scott*

While the holding in *Dred Scott*, that free blacks were not citizens and had no standing to sue in federal court, has been invalidated by ratification of the Fourteenth Amendment in 1868, the case still sheds light on what the Second Amendment meant to the Supreme Court. The Court's majority opinion warned that if blacks were recognized as *"citizens"* they would have the Constitutional right to freely travel, speak freely, hold public meetings, "and to keep and carry arms wherever they went."[37]

Recognizing that many Southern states did not consider even free blacks to be citizens of the states themselves, Justice Taney's conclusion that they were not citizens of the United States as a nation was not surprising in antebellum America. For example, one of the earliest laws in Virginia simply stated: *"all such free Mulattoes, Negroes and Indians ... shall appear without arms"*.[38] Similarly, the North Carolina Su-

---

[36] *United States v. Miller*, 307 U.S. 174 (1939).

[37] *Dred Scott v. Sandford*, 60 U.S. 393, 417 (1857). A more detailed discussion of *Dred Scott* may be found at David B. Kopel, *The Second Amendment in the Nineteenth Century*, 1998 BYU L. REV. 1359, 1433-1435 (1998).

[38] *See*, Stefan B. Tahmassebi, *Gun Control and Racism*, Geo. Mason U. Civ. Rts. L.J. 61 (1991), *citing* 7 The Statutes at Large, Being a Collection of all the Laws of Virginia, from the First Session of the Legislature, in the Year 1619 at 95 (W.W. Henning ed. 1823).

preme Court upheld a state law requiring a license for free blacks to keep or carry arms finding that, although this individual right extended to all citizens, free blacks were not citizens.[39]

As a consequence of the *Dred Scott* decision, anti-slavery activists argued that the institution of slavery, which prevented a certain class of people from bearing arms, was repugnant to the Second Amendment, which guaranteed the right to bear arms to all persons.[40]

B. Cruikshank

Mr. Cruikshank and others were tried for lynching two blacks. A sixteen count indictment was handed down against over one hundred individuals under section 6 of the Enforcement Act of 1870.[41] The indictment alleged that the defendants conspired to "hinder and prevent" two black citizens from exercising certain "rights and privileges."[42] Among them were the "lawful right and privilege to peaceably assemble together with each other and with other citizens of the United States for a peaceable and lawful purpose" and the right of "bearing arms for a lawful purpose." [43]

The Court held that the guarantees in the Bill of Rights operate to restrain governments, and not on individuals. Since there was no "state action" involved in the case, the federal courts ... could not offer relief against defendants accused of conspiracy to deprive complainants of their freedom of action and their firearms, for these violations were common-law crimes actionable only at the local level.[44]

---

[39] *State v. Newsom,* 27 N.C. (5 Ired.) 203 (1844).

[40] David B. Kopel, *The Second Amendment in the Nineteenth Century,* 1998 BYU L. REV. 1359, 1436-1441 (1998).

[41] Enforcement Act of 1870, 16 Stat. 141 (1870)

[42] *United States v. Cruikshank,* 92 U.S. 542, 548 (1875).

[43] *Id.,* at 551-553.

[44] Stephen Halbrook, That Every Man Be Armed: The Evolution of a Constitutional Right 159 (1984).

Neither the First Amendment nor the Second Amendment were among the "privileges and immunities" of United States citizenship, the court explained, because *neither* right was created by virtue of United States citizenship. In contrast to rights (such as the right to interstate travel) which were created by the Constitution, the right to assembly and the right to arms were inherent individual rights that predated the Constitution:

The right of the people peaceably to assemble for lawful purposes existed long before the adoption of the Constitution of the United States. In fact, it is, and always has been, one of the attributes of citizenship under a free government. It "derives its source," to use the language of Chief Justice Marshall, in *Gibbons v. Ogden*, 9 Wheat. 211, "from those laws whose authority is acknowledged by civilized man throughout the world." It is found wherever civilization exists. It was not, therefore, a right granted to the people by the Constitution. The government of the United States when established found it in existence, with the obligation on the part of the States to afford it protection.[45]

The Court then explained that the Second Amendment was, in this regard, the same as the First:

> The right there specified is that of "bearing arms for a lawful purpose." This is not a right granted by the Constitution. Neither is it in any manner dependent upon that instrument for its existence. The second amendment declares that it shall not be infringed; but this, as has been seen, means no more than that it shall not be infringed by Congress. [46]

Consequently, like the people's right of assembly, the right to keep and bear arms is not dependent on

---

[45] *Cruikshank* at 551.

[46] *Id.* at 591-592.

the Constitution because it preexisted the Constitution as one of the universal attributes of civilized society.[47]

C. *Presser*

Presser was the Supreme Court's first case involving a direct challenge to a statute alleged to violate the Second Amendment.[48] Presser was charged with violating an Illinois statute that made it a crime for "any body of men" other than "the regular organized volunteer militia of [Illinois], and the troops of the United States, to associate themselves together as a military company, or organization, or to drill or parade with arms" in the cities or towns of Illinois without a license of the Governor, who had unlimited authority to revoke that license.[49] In September of 1879, Presser and 400 fellow members of a labor society calling itself Lehr und Wehr Verein, marched without gubernatorial license in the streets of Chicago.[50] Presser was convicted and fined ten dollars.[51] Presser complained that this law of Illinois had the effect of depriving him of his Second Amendment right to keep and bear arms.[52]

The Supreme Court answered that the right to gather as a military group and hold armed parades was not included in the individual right to keep and bear arms.[53] The Court further expounded that "the amendment is a limitation only upon the power of Congress and the National government, and not upon that of the States."[54]

---

[47] As discussed in Part II A., *supra*, Madison himself went further, and said that both rights exist in a state of nature.

[48] *Presser v. Illinois*, 116 U.S. 252 (1886).

[49] *Id*. at 253

[50] *Id*. at 254-55.

[51] *Id*. at 254.

[52] *Id*. at 264.

[53] *Id*. at 264.

[54] *Id*. at 265.

Thus, *Presser* recognized the Second Amendment as a limitation on the power of the Federal Government. According to the court, Presser had two problems: he was raising a claim against a government (the State of Illinois) which was not bound by the Second Amendment; and the law in question (a restriction on mass armed parades) did not infringe upon the Second Amendment.[55] However, the Court *never* suggested that Mr. Presser himself had no personal Second Amendment rights. The point of the *Presser* case is that the Second Amendment right is a private right that belongs to the individual, although all rights are not unlimited.

V.   CONCLUSION

In arguing for his private Bill of Rights, Madison said:

> If they are incorporated into the constitution, independent tribunals of justice will consider themselves in a peculiar manner the guardians of those rights; they will be an impenetrable bulwark against every assumption of power in the legislative or executive; they will be naturally let to resist every encroachment upon rights expressly stipulated for in the constitution by the declaration of rights.[56]

The history of Madison's *"private rights"* amendment, the text of the Second Amendment and the few direct Supreme Court pronouncements[57] clearly sup-

---

[55] *Id.* at 264-265.

[56] House of Representatives Debates, June 8, 1789, *Schwartz* at 1016-1042.

[57] There is also a great deal of dicta supporting an individual right to keep and bear arms. SAF posted 49 Supreme Court cases on our website involving the Second Amendment/Right to Keep and Bear Arms at <http://www.saf.org/2ndAmendSupremeCourtTable.html> as part of our legal issues website

port the District Court's conclusion that the right to keep and bear arms is an individual right. The decision of the District Court should be AFFIRMED.

featuring numerous court cases, law review articles, and important quotes at <http://www.saf.org/legal-issues.html>.

 # Citizens Committee for the Right to Keep and Bear Arms

The following is a copy of the amicus curiae brief filed by the Citizens Committee for the Right to Keep and Bear Arms in support of Justice Cumming's ruling that the Lautenberg Amendment is unconstitutional. This filing argues that the United State Congress had continually legislated that the right to keep and bear arms is an individual right.

The Citizens Committee for the Right to Keep and Bear Arms is a national grassroots organization dedicated to preserving the individual right to keep and bear arms as enumerated and codified under the Second Amendment and numerous State Constitutional protections. The Citizens Committee works to educate lawmakers on the federal, state and local levels on the importance of protecting individual gun ownership and our Constitutional heritage and maintains a Washington, D.C. office for contacting all members of Congress. Fifty-eight current Members of Congress sit on the Citizens Committee National Advisory Board. The Citizens Committee represents over 650,000 members and supporters nationwide with members in every state of the union. More information is available at www.ccrkba.org

TABLE OF AUTHORITIES

CONSTITUTION AND STATUTES

10 U.S.C. § 311
10 U.S.C. § 311(a)
18 U.S.C. § 922(g)(8)
18 U.S.C. § 922(g)(9)
Brady Law of 1993
Consumer Product Safety Improvement Act of 1976 [Pub. L. 94-284, Sec. 3(e), May 11, 1976, 90 Stat. 504]
Federal Firearms Act of 1938 [Ch. 850, 52 stat. 1250 (1938)]
Firearms Owner Protection Act of 1986
Freedmen's Bureau Act of 1866 [14 Stat. 176 (1866)]
Gun Control Act of 1968
Property Requisition Act, ch. 445, 55 Stat. 742 (1941)
National Firearms Act of 1934 [48 Stat. 1236 (1934)]
U.S. Const. amend. XIV, § 1.

CASES

Cases v. U.S., 131 F.2d 916 at 922-923 (1st Cir. 1942)
Hickman v. Block, 81 F.3d 98 (9th Cir. 1996)
Perpich v. Dept. of Defense, 496 U.S. 334 (1990)
U.S. v. Emerson, 46 F.Supp.2d 598 (N.D. Tex. 1999)
U.S. v. Ficke, 58 F.Supp. 2d 1071 (D. Neb. 1999)
U.S. v. Gomez, 92 F.3d 770 (9th Cir., 1996).
U.S. v. Miller, 307 U.S. 174 (1939)
U.S. v. Panter, 688 F.2d 268 (5th Cir., 1982)

LEGISLATIVE HISTORY AND OTHER HISTORICAL SOURCES

79 Cong. Rec. 11973 (1935) Cong. Globe, 39th Cong., 1st Sess. 2764 (1866)
Documentary History of the Ratification of the Constitution, Vol. 2, Pages 508-509 (December 6, 1787)
Federalist Paper # 29, Alexander Hamilton
H.R. Rep. No. 1120, 77th Cong., 1st Sess. 2 (1941)
H.R. Report No. 141, 73d Cong., 1st sess. at (1933).
George Mason, Virginia Convention Debates of June 16,

1788 [Reprinted in Jonathan Elliot, ed, Vol. 3, The Debates in the Several State Conventions, at 425-426 (1941)]
Letter from Thomas Jefferson to Giovanni Fabbroni, June 8, 1778
Letter from Thomas Jefferson to Destutt de Tracy, January 26, 1811
Letters from the Federal Farmer to the Republic, Richard Henry Lee, Letter XVIII, May, 1788.
National Firearms Act: Hearings on H.R. 9066, Before the House Committee on Ways and Means, 73d Cong., 2d Sess. 19 (1934)
S. Rep. No. 82, 75th Cong., 1st Sess. 1-2 (1937)
Thoughts on Government, John Adams (1776)
Writings of Sam Adams, Vol III, 251 (1906).

LAW REVIEW ARTICLES AND OTHER SOURCES

Congress Interprets the Second Amendment: Declarations by a Co-Equal Branch on the Individual Right to Keep and Bear Arms, Stephen P. Halbrook, 62 Tenn. L. Rev. 597 (1995).
"Husband Murders Wife Disarmed by Police," *Women & Guns*, November (1994).
Justice Hugo Black, *The Bill of Rights*, N.Y. University Law Review, 35 at 873-74 (1960)
Monthly Vital Statistics Report, Vol. 46, No. 12 (July 28, 1998),
U.S. National Center for Health Statistics,
Statistical Abstract for the United States 1998, U.S. National Center for Health Statistics
The Right to Keep and Bear Arms, Report of the Senate Judiciary Committee Subcommittee on the Constitution, 97th Cong., 2d Sess., Committee Print I-IX, 1-23 (1982).
Virginia on Guard: Civilian Defense and the State Militia in the Second World War, Marvin W. Schlegel, (1949)
"Woman Kills Abuser Breaking Into Home," *The Pilot*, South Pines, North Carolina newspaper, Vol. 79, No. 14 (12/17/1998).

GUN RIGHTS AFFIRMED

INTRODUCTION

A. Argument Summary

Section 18 U.S.C. § 922(g)(8)[1] is unconstitutional under the Second and Fifth Amendments. First, there is no due process under this rarely used law or "notice" of substantial penalties awaiting an unsuspecting person. Second, this court should affirm the District Court's decision which has already been followed by *U.S. v. Ficke*, 58 F. Supp. 2d 1071, 1073 (D. Neb. 1999) which found 18 U.S.C. § 922(g)(9) unconstitutional. Third, there is no requirement of a judicial finding, creating an overly broad statute that casts a wide net far beyond Dr. Emerson. Fourth, this law could decrease public safety, as victims are disarmed as part of unstandardized court orders, particularly "mutual restraining orders". Fifth, Congress has repeatedly held that the Second Amendment is an individual right and it is time for this Court to uphold this individual right.

B. Factual Background

Unlike the previous classes of people prohibited from firearm ownership (people convicted of certain crimes, dishonorably discharged from the military, drug/alcohol addicts, and the adjudicated mentally-incompetent) 922(g)(8) includes prohibitions where no crime has been committed and no mental competency finding nor threat assessment is required. The court is only considering a dissolution of marriage. Dr. Emerson was charged under an "obscure, highly technical statute."[2] While 922(g)(8) is rarely used, Constitutional questions abound. This brief illustrates why 922(g)(8) is unconstitutional on Fifth and Second Amendment grounds.

---

[1] Hereinafter 922(g)(8).

[2] *U.S. v. Emerson*, 46 F.Supp.2d 598, 613 (N.D. Tex. 1999).

I. FIFTH AMENDMENT VIOLATION

C. Emerson - 18 U.S.C. § 922(g)(8)

Section 922(g)(8) violates due process under the Fifth Amendment. The government argues that Dr. Emerson received "notice" that he could not possess firearms if a restraining order was issued against him. The problems with this reasoning are multifaceted.

1. Dr. Emerson legally purchased the Beretta pistol in 1997 and correctly filled out the Form 4473 by truthfully answering "no" to the question on restraining orders.

2. Form 4473 includes many technical provisions presenting problems for understanding each subsection. While the government contends Dr. Emerson is responsible for every little detail on this four-page, small-type document, it is unreasonable to ask someone to recall all details over a year later for even a simpler form, such a rental car agreement. Moreover, unlike a car rental agreement, Dr. Emerson was not given a copy of Form 4473 for future review.

3. Even if Dr. Emerson read Form 4473 thoroughly and memorized every detail, it NEVER informed him that he must get rid of his existing firearms. The relevant portions read:

> j. Are you subject to a court order restraining you from harassing, stalking, or threatening an intimate partner or child of such partner? (See Important Notice 6...)

> IMPORTANT NOTICES...
> 6. Under 18 U.S.C. 992, firearms may not be sold to or received by persons subject to a court order...[emphasis added]

Dr. Emerson was never informed by *either Form 4473 or by the court* that he must remove his previously and legally-owned firearms or face substantial federal felony penalties (if and when he became subject to a restraining order). It is a gross distortion of our justice system to claim that any person had "fair notice" of this law under such circumstances. Therefore, 922(g)(8) is an unconstitutional Fifth Amendment violation.

D. Fricke - 18 U.S.C. § 922(g)(9)

In *U.S. v. Ficke*, the defendant was charged with violating subsection 18 U.S.C. § 922(g)(9) which makes it unlawful for any person "convicted in any court of a misdemeanor crime of domestic violence" to possess a firearm.[3] Fricke argued that 922(g)(9) violated the notice and fair warning requirements of the due process clause of the U.S. Constitution.

In 1994, Fricke entered a *pro se* plea of *no contest* to a charge of misdemeanor domestic violence assault and was sentenced to six-months probation and ordered to complete anger-control classes. Over four-years later, he was arrested at his home after his wife reported an alleged domestic assault.[4] At the home, officers found and confiscated various rifles even though nobody claimed the alleged assault involved any guns.[5] Fricke was indicted and pleaded guilty, although the court allowed a motion to dismiss before sentencing in light of the *Emerson* ruling.[6]

Fricke argued that it is fundamentally unfair to punish him for violating 922(g)(9) when: 1) his conduct in possessing the firearms was "wholly passive," and 2) he did not know that federal law proscribed his possession of firearms.[7] In granting that motion, the court found that 922(g)(9) created an impermissible strict liability crime that violates fundamental due process principles of notice and fair warning. The court concluded:

---

[3] *U.S. v. Ficke*, 58 F. Supp. 2d 1071 (D. Neb. 1999).

[4] *Id.*, at 1072.

[5] *Id.* at 1072.

[6] *Id.* at 1072.

[7] *Id.*, at 1074.

Section 922(g)(9) criminalizes behavior that for two years following this defendant's misdemeanor conviction was entirely innocent under both federal and state law. The defendant therefore received no warning during the underlying misdemeanor proceedings, at which he appeared *pro se*, that continued possession of his hunting weapons would subject him to a federal felony prosecution. The defendant had no actual notice of the enactment of this obscure, hard-to-find provision, nor would he have had a reasonable opportunity to discover it. [8]

The same rationale should compel this court to find that 922(g)(8) unconstitutionally imposes strict criminal liability when the defendant "simply did not know and did not receive fair warning that his conduct had become unlawful."[9]

II.   SECOND AMENDMENT VIOLATION

The burden of proof in civil proceedings is much lower than in criminal cases, yet the consequences under 922(g)(8) are severe. This law does not even require a judicial finding of fact to deny an individual's right to keep and bear arms. Therefore, no standards exist for termination of this right guaranteed under the Second Amendment, and of the means to exercise the right of self-defense as recognized in all courts and guaranteed under the Ninth Amendment. These fact-less, baseless grounds of deprivation contrasts sharply with other prohibited categories.

A. No Judicial Finding Required for Loss of Right to Keep and Bear Arms

The Government suggests that Dr. Emerson posed a "credible threat" to his wife's boyfriend, his wife, and his daughter. While this evidence might be relevant if the statute in question required any type of

---

[8] *Id.*, at 1075.

[9] *Id.* at 1075

judicial finding of threat, the fact is that the law was ruled unconstitutional *because* the law does not require any such evidence or finding. By trying to justify the law with allegations of threatening behavior, the government proves Judge Cumming's assertion that it is not difficult, or unreasonable, to require such evidence, and that 922(g)(8) is unconstitutional for failing to limit its scope to credible threats.

Assuming, for a moment, all the Government's allegations against Dr. Emerson are true, then he would fit into any properly narrowed statute barring firearm possession from people subject to a restraining order with a finding that the individual posed a "credible threat." Judge Cummings held that such a revised statute "would not be so offensive."[10]

The only other reason for government's inclusion of such statements about Dr. Emerson is to influence this Court against him. The vast majority of constitutional case law has been built upon individuals with less than ideal personal histories, as the Prosecution has found these persons' rights easier to violate. Dr. Emerson is entitled to the same respect for his constitutional rights as was accorded to Mr. Miranda, Mr. Escobar, Mr. Lopez, and other imperfect individuals whose rights were violated. While examining Dr. Emerson's alleged conduct is an interesting aside, it is irrelevant when considering the constitutionality of the statute. The real issue is the broad scope of the act.

B. Potentially Affects Millions Of Citizens Per Year

Section 922(g)(8) was ruled overly-broad, and a Second Amendment violation, based on the immense number of people entrapped into criminal activity -- not because of Dr. Emerson's particular circumstances. From 1975-1997, the U.S. averaged more

---

[10] *Supra* Note 2, *Emerson* at 611.

than 1 million divorces each year.[11] In 1997 alone, there were over 870,597 divorces, providing over 1,741,194 opportunities for either party to request a restraining order that would automatically bar all firearms from the person(s) subject to such orders. Divorce can include emotional rhetoric and retaliatory actions. Examples include depletion of jointly held bank accounts, incursion of substantial credit card debt, and unfounded allegations of domestic abuse and even child abuse. Allowing an automatic ban on firearms possession without any judicial finding of a fact is a violation of an individual's Second Amendment rights.

C. Decreasing Public Safety by Disarming Victim

The number of people prohibited from owning guns by civil court orders is likely to escalate as states consider "mutual restraining orders." In cases of actual domestic violence, mutual restraining orders automatically bar gun possession from both the perpetrator and the victim under 922(g)(8). Disarming victims is a tragic and unforeseen side effect of 922(g)(8) because of its unconstitutionally broad provisions. In answer to the often-repeated comment about saving women's lives through gun control, the following two brief examples illustrate the danger of 922(g)(8).

Barbara Thompson had a restraining order on an ex-boyfriend named Leotis Martin, who had previously assaulted and broke her arm and was under a court order to stay away from Barbara and her property after a break-in. Martin broke in again and was killed by his intended victim. Richmond County Sheriff Dale Furr described the events:

> ...Thompson was ... watching television when she heard the back door being broken down. She suspected it was Martin, and she ran

---

[11] *Statistical Abstract for the United States 1998* and the *Monthly Vital Statistics Report*, Vol. 46, No. 12 (July 28, 1998), U.S. National Center for Health Statistics, (1999).

immediately to the bedroom door, locked it,
and grabbed her revolver ... He kicked down
the bedroom door, fired a shot at her and
missed, and she fired back at him and didn't
miss.[12]

While the court order did not disarm the attacker,
it would have likely disarmed the intended victim if
mutual orders were granted without any judicial finding of fact. Such events prove disastrous for women.
Polly Przybyl was disarmed by the Cheektowaga, New
York police after Lee, her estranged husband of 17-
years, tracked her to her mother's home and attempted to gain entrance. The police took Ms. Przybyl's firearms even though she had called the police;
and she had both a pistol permit and a Federal Firearms License. She told the police that her husband
had guns without the necessary permits and that she
was in grave danger. Two days later, she obtained a
restraining order, but the police failed to collect his
firearms. On August 22, 1994, Lee returned, walked
to the back of the house with Polly, where he stabbed
her with a knife and killed her. Lee then retrieved a
rifle and shot Polly's mother. Lee shot himself hours
later while police were negotiating his surrender.[13]
Polly's sister, Mindy stated:

I resent that the police disarmed my sister...
Even though I personally don't believe in
guns my sister knew how to protect herself
with a gun. I believe she could have saved
herself and our mother had she been armed...
If she had a gun at least she and my mother
would have had a chance.[14]

---

[12] Woman Kills Abuser Breaking Into Home, *The Pilot* Newspaper of
South Pines, North Carolina, Vol. 79, No. 14 (12/17/1998).

[13] *Husband Murders Wife Disarmed by Police*, Women & Guns (November), p 10-11 & 55, 1994).

[14] *Id*. at 10.

The policy of disarming the victim led to the murders of Polly and her mother.

Disarming victims not only violates their right to keep and bear arms under the Second Amendment, but by extension, their means to self-protection as recognized by every court and guaranteed by the Ninth Amendment. So paramount is the right of self-defense/self-preservation, that convicted felons may raise it at trial for unlawful possession of a firearm.[15]

In *Gomez*, the Second Amendment is discussed by all three Judges. Judge Kozinski in *Footnote Seven* stated:

The Second Amendment embodies the right to defend oneself and one's home against physical attack.[16]

While separately concurring, Judge Hall stated "he would not join" *Footnote Seven*. [17] while Judge Hawkins stated that it, "alludes to an interesting and difficult question I would leave for another day."[18]

While Mrs. Przybyl's particular tragedy was caused by a strict and in this case one-sided policy of removing firearms from domestic violence situations, including from victims, and not through a restraining order under 922(g)(8), it illustrates the dangers of eliminating the individual right to keep and bear arms without requiring judicial findings of fact.

The automatic prohibition of all gun ownership through a civil court marriage-dissolution proceeding is not comparable to a person convicted of a crime, dishonorably discharged, or mentally incompetent. No prohibiting conduct must be alleged, only the issuance

---

[15] See, e.g., *U.S. v. Panter*, 688 F.2d 268 (5th Cir., 1982); *U.S. v. Gomez*, 92 F.3d 770 (9th Cir., 1996).

[16] *Gomez* at 774.

[17] *Gomez*, at 778.

[18] Gomez, at 779.

of a restraining order without any finding of fact.

Like Emerson and Fricke, most people are not likely to object to a restraining order with a potential ex-spouse when no information is provided regarding elimination of Constitutional rights and felony penalties upon the order's issuance. As written, 922(g)(8) entraps people into becoming federal felons upon leaving the courthouse. Constitutional rights should not be vacated so easily, especially without any knowledge provided.

III.   Congress Interprets the Second Amendment

This court should interpret 922(g)(8) in a manner that protects the individual right to keep and bear arms because Congress has consistently endorsed such an interpretation of the Second Amendment, as well as repeatedly supported individual firearm ownership in general. These endorsements include: the Freedmen's Bureau Act of 1866, approval of the Fourteenth Amendment, the National Firearms Act of 1934, the Federal Firearms Act of 1938, the 1941 Private Property Acquisition Act, the 1968 Gun Control Act, the Consumer Product Safety Act of 1976, the current Militia Law, The Report of the Subcommittee on the Constitution in 1982, the Firearms Owner Protection Act of 1986, and the Brady Law of 1993.[19]

A. The Freedmen's Bureau Act of 1866 and the Fourteenth Amend.

After the Civil War, slavery was ended and Southern States enacted slave codes, which made it illegal for freemen to exercise basic civil rights; including the right to purchase, own and carry firearms.[20] Congress

---

[19] See Stephen P. Halbrook, Congress Interprets the Second Amendment: Declarations by a Co-Equal Branch on the Individual Right to Keep and Bear Arms, 62 Tenn. L. Rev. 597 (1995) for more information.

[20] Norman Chachkin, History of Constitutional Litigation for Human Rights Issues--Especially Race Issues 5-7 (Practicing Law Institute, 1994).

responded to this challenge twice through the passage of the Freedmen's Bureau Act and the Fourteenth Amendment.

The Freedmen's Act read in part:

> the right ... to have full and equal benefit of all laws and proceedings concerning personal liberty, personal security, and the acquisition, enjoyment, and disposition of estate, real and personal, including the constitutional right to bear arms, shall be secured to and enjoyed by all the citizens of such State or district without respect to race or color or previous condition of slavery. [21]

Congress enacted this law through a veto override of more than two-thirds. This same two-thirds also adopted the Fourteenth Amendment, which states:

> No State shall make or enforce any law which shall abridge the privileges or immunities of citizens of the United States; nor shall any State deprive any person of life, liberty, or property, without due process of law...[22]

Senator Jacob Howard, when introducing the Fourteenth amendment, explained that its purpose was to protect "personal rights," including "the right to keep and bear arms," from infringement by the States. [23] Eighty years after the ratification of the Second Amendment, more than two-thirds of Congress believed with certainty that the Second Amendment enumerated an individual right; enough to include it in both an Act and an Amendment designed to protect the civil rights of individuals formerly held as slaves.

---

[21] 14 Stat. 176-77 (1866).

[22] U.S. Const. amend. XIV, § 1.

[23] *Cong. Globe*, 39th Cong., 1st Sess. 2764-65 (1866).

B. The National Firearms Act of 1934 (NFA)

Almost seventy years later, Congress began to consider what became the NFA.[24] The NFA, through a system of taxation and registration, severely restricted machineguns, short-barreled shotguns and rifles.[25]

Before passage of the NFA, there was detailed discussion between the Attorney General and lawmakers as to how to pass the law without violating the Second Amendment. These discussions illustrate that lawmakers considered the Second Amendment an individual right. During one crucial hearing discussion, Congressman David J. Lewis inquired about reconciling the bill with the Second Amendment's individual right to keep and bear arms:

> MR. LEWIS: Lawyer though I am, I have never quite understood how the laws of the various States have been reconciled with the provision in our Constitution denying the privilege to the legislature to take away the right to carry arms. Concealed-weapon laws, of course, are familiar in the various States; there is a legal theory upon which we prohibit the carrying of weapons--the smaller weapons.

> ATTORNEY GENERAL CUMMINGS: Do you have any doubt as to the power of the Government to deal with machine guns as they are transported in interstate commerce?

> MR. LEWIS: I hope the courts will find no doubt on a subject like this, General; but I was curious to know how we escaped that provision in the Constitution.

---

[24] 48 Stat. 1236 (1934).

[25] *Id.*

ATTORNEY GENERAL CUMMINGS: Oh, we do not attempt to escape it. We are dealing with another power, namely, the power of taxation, and of regulation under the interstate commerce clause. You see, if we made a statute absolutely forbidding any human being to have a machine gun, you might say there is some constitutional question involved. But when you say, "We will tax the machine gun," and when you say that "the absence of a license showing payment of the tax has been made indicates that a crime has been perpetrated," you are easily within the law.

MR. LEWIS: In other words, it does not amount to prohibition, but allows of regulation.

ATTORNEY GENERAL CUMMINGS: That is the idea. We have studied that very carefully. [26]

Throughout the debates, it is clear that there was a careful respect for the Second Amendment and concern about having the NFA written to include any unconstitutional infringement upon the individual right to keep and bear arms.

C. The Federal Firearms Act of 1938 (FFA)

In 1938, Congress again undertook firearms issues by passing the FFA, which regulated interstate commerce in firearms and prohibited possession of firearms by felons where an interstate nexus could be demonstrated.[27] The FFA raised concerns over the

---

[26] NFA: Hearings on H.R. 9066, House Ways and Means Committee, 73d Cong., 2d Sess. 19 (1934)

[27] FFA, Ch. 850, 52 stat. 1250 (1938).

infringement of rights guaranteed by the Second Amendment as well as highlighted Congressional support for individual gun ownership. In the early discussions on Second Amendment limitations, Senator William King stated to Senator Copeland, the chief sponsor, that "we have a constitutional provision that right of the people to keep and bear arms shall not be infringed ... [and he] was wondering if this bill was not in contravention of the constitutional provision."

> Denying that the FFA infringed upon the Second Amendment, Copeland argued that [t]he part relating to militia is important ... [as the] first part of the constitutional provision.
> Senator McKellar responded,
> while [the Second Amendment] refers to the militia, the provision is all-inclusive and provides that the right of the people to keep and bear arms shall remain inviolate.[28]

Since the FFA related to regulation of Interstate Commerce, not individual gun ownership, little more mention to the individual right to keep and bear arms under Second Amendment protection was discussed. In support of individual gun ownership, the Senate Committee explained that the FFA was designed to impact criminals, not law-abiding citizens:

> The bill under consideration...is designed to regulate the manufacture of and the shipment through interstate commerce of all firearms. ...It is believed that the bill above referred to will go far in the direction we are seeking and will eliminate the gun from the crooks' hands, while interfering as little as possible with the law-abiding citizen from whom protests have been received against

---

[28] 79 Cong. Rec. 11973 (1935).

any attempt to take from him his means of protection from the outlaws who have rendered living conditions unbearable in the past decade.[29]

D. The Property Requisition Act of 1941 (PRA)

Congress asserted the Second Amendment as an individual right by exempting privately-owned firearms from the PRA. Less than two months before Pearl Harbor, Congress passed legislation authorizing Presidential requisition of many properties with military uses from the private sector upon payment of fair compensation. [30]

Protections for Second Amendment rights were included in the PRA:

> That whenever the President, during the national emergency declared by the President on May 27, 1941, but not later than June 30, 1943, determines that (1) the use of any military or naval equipment, supplies, or munitions, or component parts thereof, or machinery, tools, or materials necessary for the manufacture, servicing, or operation of such equipment, supplies, or munitions is needed for the defense of the United States; (2) such need is immediate and impending and such as will not admit of delay or resort to any other source of supply; and (3) all other means of obtaining the use of such property for the defense of the United States upon fair and reasonable terms have been exhausted, he is authorized to requisition such property for the defense of the United States upon the payment of fair and just compensation for

---

[29] S. Rep. No. 82, 75th Cong., 1st Sess. 1-2 (1937).

[30] PRA, ch. 445, 55 Stat. 742 (1941).

> such property to be determined as hereinafter provided, and to dispose of such property in such manner as he may determine is necessary for the defense of the United States....
> Nothing contained in this Act shall be construed-
> to authorize the requisitioning or require the registration of any firearms possessed by any individual for his personal protection or sport (and the possession of which is not prohibited or the registration of which is not required by existing law),
> to impair or infringe in any manner the right of any individual to keep and bear arms, or
> to authorize the requisitioning of any machinery or equipment which is in actual use in connection with any operating factory or business and which is necessary to the operation of such factory or business.[31]

Originally, the bill did not include language protecting the individual right to keep and bear arms, but the House Military Affairs Committee added these provisions, noting:

> It is not contemplated or even inferred that the President, or any executive board, agency, or officer, would trespass upon the right of the people in this respect. There appears to be no occasion for the requisition of firearms owned and maintained by the people for sport and recreation, nor is there any desire or intention on the part of the Congress or the President to impair or infringe the right of the people under section 2 of the Constitution of the United States, which reads, in part, as follows: "the right of the people to keep and bear arms shall not be infringed." However, in view of the fact that certain totalitarian and dictatorial nations are now engaged in the willful and wholesale destruction of personal rights and liberties, your committee deem[s] it appropriate for the Con-

---

[31] PRA, ch. 445, 55 Stat. 742 (1941) [emphasis added].

gress to expressly state that the proposed legislation shall not be construed to impair or infringe the constitutional right of the people to bear arms. In so doing, it will be manifest that, although the Congress deems it expedient to grant certain extraordinary powers to the Executive in furtherance of the common defense during critical times, there is no disposition on the part of this Government to depart from the concepts and principles of personal rights and liberties expressed in our Constitution.[32]

This provision was essential for the preservation of the individual right to keep and bear arms because if private guns were registered, the government could confiscate them. Compare the retention of private guns with the plight of the organized portion of the militia. The War Department began taking back all the rifles it had previous issued to them.[33] If, as the Government contends, the entire militia is only the "select" militia (the National Guard), then the Second Amendment is the first guarantee of the Bill of Rights to cease to exist. Under the PRA, the organized portion of the militia was disarmed and could be again.

C. The Current Militia Law of 1956

Congress currently defines the militia under Title 10, Chapter 13 of the U.S. Code.
Sec. 311. Militia: composition and classes
(a) The militia of the United States consists of all able-bodied males at least 17 years of age and, except as provided in section 313 of title 32, under 45 years of age who are, or who have made a declaration of intention to become, citizens of the United States and of female citizens of
the United States who are members of the National Guard.

---

[32] H.R. Rep. No. 1120, 77th Cong., 1st Sess. 2 (1941) [emphasis added].

[33] See, e.g., Marvin W. Schlegel, Virginia on Guard: Civilian Defense and the State Militia in the Second World War at 129 (1949).

> (b) The classes of the militia are —
> the organized militia, which consists of the
> National Guard and the Naval Militia; and
> the unorganized militia, which consists of the
> members of the militia who are not members
> of the National Guard or the Naval Militia.
> [emphasis added]

Dr. Emerson is between the ages of 17 through 45 and is therefore part of the militia as defined under current law by Congress. This definition is also supported by the Supreme Court in *U.S. v. Miller*,[34] which reads:

The signification attributed to the term Militia appears from the debates in the Convention, the history and legislation of Colonies and States, and the writings of approved commentators. These show plainly enough that the Militia comprised all males physically capable of acting in concert for the common defense. "A body of citizens enrolled for military discipline." And further, that ordinarily when called for service these men were expected to appear bearing arms supplied by themselves and of the kind in common use at the time.[35]

Applying this very narrow definition under Section 311(a) (which may be gender biased and discriminatory by today's standards), Dr. Emerson qualifies as part of the militia. Although he is currently not called into active service, according to *Miller*, he can "keep" his Beretta 92 pistol, which is identical to the one issued in the Armed Forces, until called to bear arms to provide for the common defense.

Congress and the Supreme Court in *Miller* concur on the definition of the militia. The Court never questioned whether Mr. Miller was part of the militia, a very troubling fact for the "collective" rights theorists. If Miller was not part of the militia to begin with, then there would be no need to examine whether the

---

[34] 307 U.S. 174 (1939).

[35] *Id.* at 818-819 [emphasis added].

firearm was a militia-type. It would have been a simple "no standing" case, similar to *Hickman v. Block*, 81 F.3d 98, 96 (9th Cir., 1996). Nobody from the "collective rights" theory has ever explained this discrepancy.[36]

Congress, along with the *Miller* Court, upheld the beliefs of the Framers of our Constitution, who were avid supporters of individual gun ownership and its protection under the Second Amendment. Many of them also detailed the value of individual firearm ownership toward "the preservation or efficiency of a well regulated militia"[37] as required under the *Miller* court and detailed under the current Militia Law. These same Framers feared the destruction of the "general militia" as defined by Congress and *Miller* and opposed the "select militia" as the Government brief supports. Some of the Framers' statements include:

> I enclose you a list of the killed, wounded, and captives of the enemy from the commencement of hostilities at Lexington in April, 1775, until November, 1777, since which there has been no event of any consequence... I think that upon the whole it has been about one half the number lost by them, in some instances more, but in others less. This difference is ascribed to our superiority in taking aim when we fire; every soldier in our army having been intimate with his gun from his infancy. [emphasis added]
> --Thomas Jefferson letter to Giovanni Fabbroni, June 8, 1778.

> A militia, when properly formed, are in fact the people themselves ... the constitution

---

[36] Contrast Government's *Miller* reading with the individual right's interpretation supported by Justice Hugo Black, *The Bill of Rights*, N.Y. University Law Review, 35 at 873 (1960) and recognized and feared in *Cases v. U.S.*, 131 F.2d 916 at 922-923 (1st Cir. 1942).

[37] *Id* at 178.

ought to secure a genuine and guard against a select militia, by providing that the militia shall always by kept well organized, armed, and disciplined, and include, according to the past and general usuage of the states, all men capable of bearing arms...
--Richard Henry Lee writing in *Letters from the Federal Farmer to the Republic*, Letter XVIII, May, 1788.

I ask, Who are the militia? They consist now of the whole people, except a few public officers.
--George Mason, 3 Elliot, *Debates* at 425-426, June 16, 1788 [38]

...their governor, constitutionally, the commander of the militia of the State, that is to say, of every man in it able to bear arms...
--Thomas Jefferson, letter to Destutt de Tracy, January 26, 1811.

The project of disciplining all the militia of the United States is as futile as it would be injurious, if it were capable of being carried into execution...Little more can reasonably be aimed at, with respect to the people at large, than to have them properly armed and equipped;...
--Alexander Hamilton, *The Federalist Papers* # 29.

A militia law, requiring all men, or with very few exceptions besides cases of conscience, to be provided with arms and ammunition... is always a wise institution, and, in the present circumstances of our country, indispensable.

---

[38] Reprinted in Jonathan Elliot, ed, Vol. 3, *The Debates in the Several State Conventions*, at 425-426 (1941)

--John Adams, Thoughts on Government, 1776.

I object to the power of Congress over the militia and to keep a standing army ... The last resource of a free people is taken away; for Congress are to have the command of the Militia ... Congress may give us a select militia which will, in fact, be a standing army--or Congress, afraid of a general militia, may say there shall be no militia at all. When a select militia is formed; the people in general may be disarmed.
--John Smilie in the Pennsylvania convention. *The Documentary History of the Ratification of the Constitution*, Vol. 2, Pages 508-509 (December 6, 1787).

The Militia is composed of free Citizens. There is therefore no Danger of their making use of their Power to the destruction of their own Rights, or suffering others to invade them.
Samuel Adams. III *S. Adams Writings* 251 (1906).

The Framers' intent was to have an armed populace capable of defending themselves from *all* forms of tyranny. Their words still ring true in both the current Militia law and the *Miller* decision. Additional history of Congress's Militia Acts is detailed in *Perpich v. Dept. of Defense*,[39] which holds that the militia under the 1903 Dick Act is:

... divided the class of able-bodied male citizens between 18 and 45 years of age into an "organized militia" to be known as the National Guard of the several States, and the remainder of which was then described as the

---

[39] 496 U.S. 334 (1990).

"reserve militia," and which later statutes have termed the "unorganized militia." [40]

Congress, *Miller*, the Framers and *Perpich* all hold that the militia is more than the State or National guard. This court should follow this long-standing interpretation.

F. Consumer Product Safety Improvement Act of 1976 (CPSIA)

When Congress authorized broad, sweeping powers to the Consumer Product Safety Commission, there was a concern that over-regulation would impact the individual gun ownership. An exemption from the law was created for the manufacture and sale of firearms or firearms ammunition. Pub. L. 94-284, Sec. 3(e), May 11, 1976, 90 Stat. 504, provided that:

> The Consumer Product Safety Commission shall make no ruling or order that restricts the manufacture or sale of firearms, firearms ammunition, or components of firearms ammunition, including black powder or gunpowder for firearms.

It is clear that this amendment was adopted specifically to protect individual gun owners from intrusive and overbearing government bureaucracy and the restrictions that could occur. Although the Consumer Product Safety Act does not specifically invoke the Second Amendment, the CPSIA does reflect Congress's strong desire to protect individual gun ownership. This Court should read 922(g)(8) in a manner that would uphold this Congressional desire.

G. Subcommittee on the Constitution, 1982

Congress clarified the meaning of the Second

---

[40] *Perpich*, 496 U.S. at 341 [emphasis added].

Amendment in the February 1982 Report of the Subcommittee on the Constitution of the Committee on the Judiciary in the 97th Congress, *The Right to Keep and Bear Arms*. This is a good summary of the meaning of the Second Amendment. (Though many additional individual rights scholarly materials were recovered since the report was issued.) It was a unanimous, bipartisan and strongly-worded Report supporting the individual right to keep and bear arms. In his opening remarks, Senator Orrin Hatch wrote:

> What the Subcommittee on the Constitution uncovered was clear --and long-lost--proof that the second amendment to our Constitution was intended as an individual right of the American citizen to keep and carry arms in a peaceful manner, for protection of himself, his family, and his freedoms. [41]

Sen. Dennis Deconcini echoed respect for the Second Amendment, quoting Thomas Jefferson and Samuel Adams and noted:

> The right to bear arms is a tradition with deep roots in American society... I have personally been disappointed that so important an issue should have generally been so thinly researched and so minimally debated both in Congress and the courts. [42]

The report then quoted Framers of our Constitution, Legal Commentators of the time, and various court cases. The concluding paragraphs destroy the notion that the "militia" is the National Guard of today and reaffirm the Second Amendment as an individual right:

---

[41] *The Right to Keep and Bear Arms*, Report of the Senate Judiciary Committee Subcommittee on the Constitution, 97th Cong., 2d Sess., P. viii.

[42] *Id.*, Page xi. See also http://www.2ndlawlib.org/journals/senrpt/senrpt.html

That the National Guard is not the "Militia" referred to in the second amendment is even clearer today. Congress has organized the National Guard under its power to "raise and support armies" and not its power to "Provide for organizing, arming and disciplining the Militia"[43] This Congress chose to do in the interests of organizing reserve military units which were not limited in deployment by the strictures of our power over the constitutional militia, which can be called forth only "to execute the laws of the Union, suppress insurrections and repel invasions." The modern National Guard was specifically intended to avoid status as the constitutional militia, a distinction recognized by 10 U.S.C. Sec 311(a).

The conclusion is thus inescapable that the history, concept, and wording of the second amendment to the Constitution of the United States, as well as its interpretation by every major commentator and court in the first half-century after its ratification, indicates that what is protected is an individual right of a private citizen to own and carry firearms in a peaceful manner.[44]

H. The Firearms Owners' Protection Act of 1986(FOPA)

Congress again supported the individual right to keep and bear arms in passing the FOPA, by finding that:

> the rights of citizens—
> to keep and bear arms under the second amendment to the United States Constitution;
> to security against illegal and unreasonable searches and seizures under the fourth amendment;

---

[43] H.R. Report No. 141, 73d Cong., 1st sess. at 2-5 (1933).

[44] *Supra.* Note 36, P. 11-12 [emphasis added].

Against uncompensated taking of property, double jeopardy, and assurance of due process of law under the Fifth Amendment; and against unconstitutional exercise of authority under the ninth and tenth amendments; require additional legislation to correct existing firearms statutes and enforcement policies; and

(2) additional legislation is required to reaffirm the intent of the Congress, as expressed in section 101 of the Gun Control Act of 1968, that "it is not the purpose of this title to place any undue or unnecessary Federal restrictions or burdens on law-abiding citizens with respect to the acquisition, possession, or use of firearms appropriate to the purpose of hunting, trap shooting, target shooting, personal protection, or any other lawful activity, and that this title is not intended to discourage or eliminate the private ownership or use of firearms by law-abiding citizens for lawful purposes." [45]

The FOPA enforces the Second Amendment protection through prevention of registration of most firearms by providing:

...No such rule or regulation prescribed after the date of the enactment of the Firearms Owners' Protection Act may require that records required to be maintained under this chapter or any portion of the contents of such records, be recorded at or transferred to a facility owned, managed, or controlled by the United States or any State or any political subdivision thereof, nor that any system of registration of firearms, firearms owners, or

---

[45] FOPA § 1(b), 100 Stat. 449 (1986) (codified at 18 U.S.C. § 921 et seq.).

firearms transactions or dispositions be established.[46]

The FOPA continued the no-registration policy of the PRA. This protection even carried over to appropriation budgets of the Bureau of Alcohol, Tobacco and Firearms (BATF). Congress has included the following provision in every BATF appropriation act since 1978:

> *Provided,* That no funds appropriated herein shall be available for administrative expenses in connection with consolidating or centralizing within the Department of the Treasury the records of receipts and disposition of firearms maintained by Federal firearms licensees or for issuing or carrying out any provisions of the proposed rules of the Department of the Treasury, Bureau of Alcohol, Tobacco and Firearms, on Firearms Regulations, as published in the Federal Register, volume 43, number 55, of March 21, 1978....[47]

I. The Brady Handgun Control Law

The Congressional prohibition on firearm/firearm-owner registration is reaffirmed again in the Brady Law. Section 103 dealing with the National Instant Criminal Background check system reads in part:

> (i) Prohibition Relating To Establishment of Registration Systems With Respect to Firearms. - No department, agency, officer, or employee of the United States may --
>
> (1) require that any record or portion thereof generated by the system established under

---

[46] 18 U.S.C. 926(3)

[47] E.g., 106 Stat. 1731 (1992).

this section be recorded at or transferred to a facility owned, managed, or controlled by the United States or any State or political subdivision thereof; or

(2) use the system established under this section to establish any system for the registration of firearms, firearm owners, or firearm transactions or dispositions, except with respect to persons, prohibited by section 922(g) or (n) of title 18, United States Code, or State law, from receiving a firearm.[48]

This portion of Brady continues the policy from the PRA and FOPA, both of which specifically protected the individual right to keep and bear arms under the Second Amendment.

J. Congressional History as a Whole

The continuous effort of Congress to avoid infringing on the individual right to keep and bear arms goes virtually unnoticed in lower court cases presuming that the Second Amendment is simply a "collective" right. It is time for the Judicial Branch to consider the long-standing opinion of the Legislative Branch in ruling on the intent behind the Second Amendment. It was first drafted, debated and ratified by Congress and has been defended rigorously as an individual right throughout our nation's history.

Particularly with an ambiguous statute like 922(g)(8), courts must consider the interpretation preferred by Congress as the crafters of the legislation. Because Congress has repeatedly acted to protect individual firearms ownership in general, and the Second Amendment in particular, the statutory interpretation that best effectuates these often-expressed preferences should be upheld.

This court should interpret the statute at bar to

---

[48] Section 103 of Pub. L. 103-159.

require a finding of dangerous not only because such a reading is consistent with the Second Amendment, but because it matches the expressions of Congressional intent regarding the Second Amendment and individual gun ownership. If such a reading is not possible, then the statute must be struck-down as an unconstitutional Second Amendment violation.

D. CONCLUSION

Section 922(g)(8), if not given a saving construction by this Court, is--like 922(g)(9)--a clear violation of both the Fifth and Second Amendments. The Judgment of the District Court should be affirmed.

National Rifle Association

The following is the amicus curiae brief filed in the Emerson case by the National Rifle Association.

The National Rifle Association of America was organized in 1871 as a not for profit corporation in accordance with New York law. It is recognized as a § 501(c)(4) entity under the Internal Revenue Code. Its mission includes protecting the right to keep and bear arms. The parties have consented to NRA's appearance by brief only.

The statute at issue in this case, 18 U.S.C. § 922(g)(8), was intended to prevent persons with a demonstrated history of domestic violence from possessing firearms while under a valid restraining order. The government now contends that the statute also applies to a pro forma order entered in a state divorce proceeding without any judicial finding that the person subject to the order had ever engaged in domestic abuse, or was likely ever to do so. The court below correctly concluded that such a sweeping and arbitrary infringement on the right to keep and bear arms violates the Second Amendment.

No court has ever approved a federal statute imposing a complete deprivation of the right to possess firearms without a particularized finding of some disabling characteristic. Nor could a court have done so, for Congress has never before enacted such a statute. The cases cited by the government in its brief all relate to restrictions on narrow categories of weapons or to settled categories of disqualified persons such as convicted felons. This Court should make no mistake about the difference between those cases and this one: the government is now asking for a radical extension of federal power when it insists on disarming law-abiding American citizens simply because they are involved in divorce proceedings.

After briefly reviewing the meaning of the Second Amendment, we will demonstrate that the case law on which the government relies does not compel this Court to adopt an interpretation of the Constitution that is at odds with its text and history.

GUN RIGHTS AFFIRMED

TABLE OF AUTHORITIES
Cases:

Constitutional and Statutory Provisions:

10 U.S.C. § 311
18 U.S.C. § 922(g)(8)
Act of May 8, 1792, ch. 33, 1 Stat. 271
Articles of Confederation art. VI, ¶ 4
U.S. Const. art. I, § 8, cl. 16

Other Authorities:

William Blackstone, *Commentaries* (St. George Tucker ed. 1803)

Thomas M. Cooley, *The General Principles of Constitutional Law in the United States of America* (2d ed. 1891)

3 J. Elliot, *Debates in the Several State Conventions* 45 (2d ed. 1836)

3 J. Elliot, *Debates in the Several State Conventions* 425 (3d ed. 1937)

Robert J. Cottrol & Raymond T. Diamond, *The Second Amendment: Toward an Afro-Americanist Reconsideration*, 80 Georgetown L.J. 309 (1991)

2 Max Farrand, *The Records of the Federal Convention* (1911)

The Federalist (C. Rossiter ed., 1961)

Don B. Kates, *The Second Amendment and the Ideology of Self-Protection*, 9 Const. Commentary 87 (1992)

Gary Kleck, *Targeting Guns: Firearms and their Control* (Aldine de Gruyter 1997)

Gary Kleck & Marc Gertz, *Armed Resistance to Crime: The Prevalence and Nature of Self-Defense with a Gun*, 86 J. Crim. L. & Criminology 150 (1995)

Sanford Levinson, *The Embarrassing Second Amendment*, 99 Yale L.J. 637 (1989)

John R. Lott, Jr., *More Guns, Less Crime: Understanding Crime and Gun Control Laws* (University of Chicago Press 1998)

Nelson Lund, *The Ends of Second Amendment Jurisprudence: Firearms Disabilities and Domestic Violence Restraining Orders*, 4 Tex. Rev. L. & Politics 157 (1999)

Nelson Lund, *The Past and Future of the Individual's Right to Arms*, 31 Ga. L. Rev. 1 (1996)

GUN RIGHTS AFFIRMED

Joyce Lee Malcolm, *To Keep and Bear Arms: The Origins of an Anglo-American Right* (Harvard University Press 1994)

William Rawle, *A View of the Constitution of the United States of America* (2d ed. 1829)

3 Joseph Story, *Commentaries on the Constitution of the United States* (1833)

Laurence H. Tribe, 1 *American Constitutional Law* (3d ed. 2000)

William Van Alstyne, *The Second Amendment and the Personal Right to Arms*, 43 Duke, L.J. 1236 (1994)

Reynolds & Kates, *The Second Amendment and States' Rights: A Thought Experiment*, 36 Wm. & Mary L. Rev. 1737 (1995)

Eugene Volokh, *The Commonplace Second Amendment*, 73 N.Y.U. L. Rev. 793 (1998)

INTEREST STATEMENT
AND IDENTITY OF AMICUS CURIAE

The National Rifle Association of America was organized in 1871 as a not for profit corporation in accordance with New York law. It is recognized as a § 501(c)(4) entity under the Internal Revenue Code. Its mission includes protecting the right to keep and bear arms. The parties have consented to NRA's appearance by brief only.

SUMMARY OF ARGUMENT

The statute at issue in this case, 18 U.S.C. § 922(g)(8), was intended to prevent persons with a demonstrated history of domestic violence from possessing firearms while under a valid restraining order. The government now contends that the statute also applies to a pro forma order entered in a state divorce proceeding without any judicial finding that the person subject to the order had ever engaged in domestic abuse, or was likely ever to do so. The court below correctly concluded that such a sweeping and arbitrary infringement on the right to keep and bear arms violates the Second Amendment.

No court has ever approved a federal statute imposing a complete deprivation of the right to possess firearms without a particularized finding of some disabling characteristic. Nor could a court have done so, for Congress has never before enacted such a statute. The cases cited by the government in its brief all relate to restrictions on narrow categories of weapons or to settled categories of disqualified persons such as convicted felons. This Court should make no mistake about the difference between those cases and this one: the government is now asking for a radical extension of federal power when it insists on disarming law-abiding American citizens simply because they are involved in divorce proceedings.[1]

---

[1] Appellee Emerson and Amicus Attorney General of Alabama present a compelling case for construing section 922(g)(8) to require a judicial find-

After briefly reviewing the meaning of the Second Amendment, we will demonstrate that the case law on which the government relies does not compel this Court to adopt an interpretation of the Constitution that is at odds with its text and history.

ARGUMENT

I. The Second Amendment protects the fundamental, individual right to keep and bear arms.

The Second Amendment provides:

> "A well regulated Militia, being necessary to the security of a free State, the right of the people to keep and bear Arms, shall not be infringed."

Notwithstanding the confusion about this text engendered by twentieth-century debates over gun control, its meaning was perfectly clear to those who framed and ratified it, and to virtually every serious legal commentator during the first century of the Constitution's existence. The Second Amendment simply forbids the federal government from infringing the right of individual American citizens to keep and bear arms, and this prohibition contributes to fostering "a well regulated militia" by preserving the armed citizenry from which the framers believed that such a militia should be drawn. Like every other provision of the Bill of Rights, the Second Amendment has its limits. But, like every other provision of the Bill of Rights, the Second Amendment must mean something. The Second Amendment will mean nothing if the government can arbitrarily disarm American citizens who have never been shown to be dangerous or irresponsible.

---

ing of dangerousness as a predicate for imposing a firearms disability. We agree that judicial restraint requires this construction of the statute, because the government's interpretation renders the statute plainly unconstitutional.

A. The text and history of the Second Amendment are consistent and unambiguous.

The Second Amendment unequivocally states that "the right of the people to keep and bear arms shall not be infringed." Modern scholarship has repeatedly and conclusively demonstrated that this is a right belonging to individuals, just like the "right[s] of the people" set out in the First and Fourth Amendments. See, e.g., Laurence H. Tribe, *1 American Constitutional Law* 902 n. 221 (2000) (Second Amendment recognizes "a right (admittedly of uncertain scope) on the part of individuals to possess and use firearms in the defense of themselves and their homes.") The Constitution's unequivocal statement is not qualified or diminished by the prefatory phrase, "A well regulated Militia, being necessary to the security of a free State . . ." Such prefatory statements of purpose were very common in state constitutions with which the framers were familiar, and they were never interpreted to detract from the operative clauses to which they were appended. Eugene Volokh, *The Commonplace Second Amendment*, 73 N.Y.U. L. Rev. 793 (1998) (discussing dozens of examples). Any attempt to use this prefatory language to recast the individual right as some sort of collective or governmental right leads to intolerable textual difficulties, and even outright absurdities. See, e.g., William Van Alstyne, *The Second Amendment and the Personal Right to Arms*, 43 Duke L.J. 1236 (1994); Nelson Lund, *The Past and Future of the Individual's Right to Arms*, 31 Ga. L. Rev. 1, 20-29 (1996); Reynolds & Kates, *The Second Amendment and States' Rights: A Thought Experiment*, 36 Wm. & Mary L. Rev. 1737 (1995).

As the constitutional text suggests, the right of the individual to keep and bear arms was closely associated by the framers with the militia tradition that the American colonists brought with them from England. Many Americans of the late eighteenth century were mistrustful of standing armies, and the Federalists and Anti-Federalists were agreed on at least one fundamental point: liberty was more secure on these shores than in England because the American people were armed. James Madison, for example, excoriated the European governments that were "afraid to trust the people with arms" and stressed "the advantage of being armed, which the Americans possess over the people of almost every other nation." *The Federalist* No. 46, at 299 (C. Rossiter, ed. 1961). Patrick Henry, who opposed ratification of the Constitution partly because he feared the specter of federal control over weapons and their use, similarly proclaimed: "The great object is that every man be armed. . . . Everyone who is able may have a gun." 3 J. Elliot, *Debates in the Several State Conventions* 45 (2d ed. 1836).

The militia tradition with which the Framers associated the right to keep and bear arms was fundamentally different from our contemporary National Guard system.[2] As the Supreme Court has recognized, the eighteenth century militia "comprised all males physically capable of acting in concert for the common defense." *United States v. Miller*, 307 U.S. 174, 179 (1939). This was not a legal definition, and in fact the Constitution provides no definition of the militia. But the legal definition adopted in the first Militia Act was perfectly consistent with the spirit of this formulation. Act of May 8, 1792, ch. 33, 1 Stat. 271 (requiring militia enrollment for most able-bodied white males between the ages of 17 and 45). To this very day, Congress has continued to define the militia so that it includes almost all men between the ages of 17 and 45. 10 U.S.C. § 311.

For the framers, the militia was always put in sharp contrast with standing military organizations of any kind. See, e.g., *Articles of Confederation* art. VI, 4; 3 J. Elliot, *Debates in the Several State Conventions* 425 (3d ed. 1937) (statement of George Mason, June 14, 1788) ("Who are the Militia? They consist now of the whole people. . . ."); Joyce Lee Malcolm, *To Keep*

---

[2] The National Guard consists of state-based military organizations whose members enlist both in their state units and in the federal armed forces. *Perpich v. Department of Defense*, 496 U.S. 334, 345 (1990).

and Bear Arms: The Origins of an Anglo-American Right 148 (Harvard University Press 1994) ("Because of their long-standing prejudice against a select militia as constituting a form of standing army liable to be skewed politically and dangerous to liberty, every state had [in the post-Revolutionary period] created a general militia."). It was hoped that government would provide military training so that the militia could operate effectively when the need arose, but this training was not a sine qua non for the existence of the militia. The essential character of the militia lay in two fundamental qualities: that it remained inactive until a need for its services arose, and that it remained armed while in its usual inactive state. See, e.g., *Miller*, 307 U.S. at 179 ("[O]rdinarily when called for service these [militia] men were expected to appear bearing arms supplied by themselves and of the kind in common use at the time.")

The purpose of the Second Amendment is not and cannot be to ensure that the militia receives adequate military training from the government. The government had already been given the power to provide for such training. U.S. Const. art. I, § 8, cl. 16. Nor does the Second Amendment purport to require that this congressional power be exercised responsibly, or indeed exercised at all. The more well-trained the militia was, the more effective it would be, and so the less often would circumstances require the raising of real armies consisting of full-time, paid troops. And since standing armies were seen as a dangerous tool that would-be tyrants might use to oppress the people, a well-trained militia was widely viewed as a desirable goal, so long as the militia retained its essentially civilian character. See, e.g., *The Federalist* No. 29, at 183 (A. Hamilton). But the Constitution gave the federal government virtually unlimited authority to raise armies, and it imposed no requirement that the militia receive effective training. See U.S. Const. art. I, § 8, cls. 12-16. The framers consciously considered and rejected a constitutional provision discouraging peacetime standing armies, and they no doubt recognized that it would be infeasible to write a constitutional rule requiring that the militia be well trained. See 2 Max Farrand, *The Records of the Federal Convention* 616-17 (1911).

What the Second Amendment does for the militia is to ensure that "the people," from which the militia must be drawn, can remain armed while the militia is in its normal, inactive state. This is why the Constitution's reference to a "well regulated militia" does not mean organizations like our National Guard. Eighteenth century readers, unfamiliar with the modern administrative state, would naturally have recognized that "well regulated" does not necessarily mean "heavily regulated." Rather, it can just as easily mean "not overly regulated" or "not inappropriately regulated." This insight is crucial to understanding the prefatory language of the Second Amendment. A "well regulated" militia is, among other things, not inappropriately regulated. The Second Amendment simply forbids one form of inappropriate regulation that the government might be especially tempted to promulgate: disarming the civilian population from which the militia must be drawn. See Nelson Lund, *The Ends of Second Amendment Jurisprudence: Firearms Disabilities and Domestic Violence Restraining Orders*, 4 Tex. Rev. L. & Politics 157 (1999). Article I authorizes the federal government to adopt a wide range of militia regulations, such as requiring civilians to possess arms and requiring them to undergo military training. See, e.g., Act of May 8, 1792, ch. 33, 1 Stat. 271. The Second Amendment is not a foolish redundancy on Article I, but an important prohibition against the one intolerable form of regulation: civilian disarmament.

B.. The right to keep and bear arms continues to serve its constitutional purpose in contemporary America.

A civilian population that is protected from the threat of disarmament contributes to "the security of a free state" in two principal ways. First, the very ex-

istence of an armed citizenry will tend to discourage
would-be tyrants from attempting to use paid troops
to "pacify" the population. This is not and could not be
a guarantee against tyranny, but it surely raises the
risks and costs of a tyrannous pacification, and
thereby reduces the probability of its being attempted.
See, e.g., Sanford Levinson, *The Embarrassing Second
Amendment*, 99 Yale L.J. 637, 657 & n.96 (1989). Second, and no less important, an armed citizenry is
much less dependent on the government for protection
from the hazards of everyday life, both in a world (like
that of the eighteenth century) where organized police
forces did not exist, and in a world (like ours) in which
the police can almost never put a stop to crimes in
progress.[3]

It may be true that we have less reason to fear
standing armies today. It is certainly true that our
reliance on the traditional militia system for national
defense and law enforcement has declined.[4] But unreasonable gun control policies could still facilitate the
tyrannical oppression of political minorities, as they
have in the past. See, e.g., Cottrol & Diamond, *The
Second Amendment: Toward an Afro-Americanist Reconsideration*, 80 Georgetown L.J. 309 (1991). And
even if one discounts such dangers, the constitutional
right to arms contributes to "the security of a free
state" in a second way.

As the Founders were well aware, the right of civilians to arm themselves enables citizens to exercise
their fundamental, natural right to self-defense when
they are threatened with criminal attack. See, e.g.,
Don B. Kates, *The Second Amendment and the Ideology of Self-Protection*, 9 Const. Commentary 87 (1992).
The most reliable studies indicate that armed civilians defend themselves against criminal violence over

---

[3] Nor is the government constitutionally obligated to prevent crime. *See,
e.g., DeShaney v. Winnebago County Department of Social Services*, 489
U.S. 189 (1989); *Saenz v. Heldenfels Brothers, Inc.*, 183 F.3d 389 (5th Cir.
1999).

[4] Article I specifically authorizes use of the militia for law enforcement.
U.S. Const. art. 1, § 8, cl. 15.

two million times each year. Gary Kleck & Marc Gertz, *Armed Resistance to Crime: The Prevalence and Nature of Self-Defense with a Gun*, 86 J. Crim. L. & Criminology 150, 164 (1995). Simply displaying a weapon is almost always sufficient to stop an attack, though armed civilians (who far outnumber the police) also shoot many more criminals than the police do. Gary Kleck, *Targeting Guns: Firearms and their Control* 162, 163 (Aldine de Gruyter 1997). In addition, the widespread civilian ownership of firearms in the United States creates powerful deterrent effects on criminal activity. Burglaries of occupied dwellings, for example, are rare in the United States compared with Canada and Great Britain. Id. at 183. The recent wave of liberalized concealed-carry laws has produced dramatic declines in violent crime in Texas and the other states that have adopted this policy. John R. Lott, Jr., *More Guns, Less Crime: Understanding Crime and Gun Control Laws* (University of Chicago Press 1998). Among the greatest beneficiaries of this policy have been women (who are more physically vulnerable than men) and minorities (who tend to live in areas where violent crime rates are higher). Id. at 60-70.

None of this implies that the Second Amendment prevents Congress from adopting reasonable measures to prevent the misuse of firearms. On the contrary, just as there are many permissible restrictions on free speech—ranging from laws against perjury and fraud, to restrictions on obscenity and child pornography—so there are numerous ways in which government may regulate exceptionally dangerous weapons and prevent dangerous persons (such as juveniles, violent felons, and the mentally ill) from possessing guns at all. But all such laws must be narrowly tailored to serve compelling public purposes, and all such laws must be subject to strict scrutiny by the courts. A statute arbitrarily imposing a complete and automatic firearms disability on a citizen who has merely been told to obey the law in a pro forma divorce court order, without any finding of past or future dangerousness, simply cannot survive constitutional scrutiny. If it could, the government would be free to impose the same disability on all Americans—any of whom might someday break the law—or on any disfavored subset of the population. If that could be done, the Second Amendment would protect only those rights that the government chose not to infringe. This absurd conclusion is inconsistent with the constitutional text and with everything the Framers said about the right to keep and bear arms.

II. SUPREME COURT PRECEDENT DOES NOT SUPPORT THE CONSTITUTIONALITY OF THE GOVERNMENT'S ATTEMPTED APPLICATION OF SECTION 922(g)(8).

The Supreme Court has issued only one opinion dealing with a Second Amendment challenge to a federal statute: *United States v. Miller*, 307 U.S. 174 (1939). Before turning to that case, we should note that the government's repeated reliance on a dictum in *Lewis v. United States*, 445 U.S. 55, 65 n.8 (1980), is entirely misplaced. The Second Amendment was not at issue in *Lewis*, which dealt with an equal-protection challenge to the federal statute forbidding felons to possess firearms. In the course of its equal-protection analysis, the Court dropped a footnote that included a passing reference to *Miller*. Although the citation to *Miller* was inapposite, the *Lewis* Court's actual decision upholding the federal felon-in-possession statute was perfectly consistent with Second Amendment protection of the rights of law-abiding citizens. As *Lewis* noted, 445 U.S. at 66, even the most fundamental of rights, like voting, can be taken away from convicted felons.

The government's extensive discussions of dicta in cases dealing with Second Amendment challenges to state laws are also misplaced. During the nineteenth century, the Supreme Court held that the Bill of Rights, including the Second Amendment, applies only to the federal government. See, e.g., *United States v. Cruikshank*, 92 U.S. 542 (1875); *Presser v. Illinois*, 116 U.S. 252 (1886). That Court has subsequently held that some parts of the Bill of Rights (but not others) also constrain state governments by virtue of "incorporation" through the Fourteenth Amendment's Due Process Clause. See, e.g., *Duncan v. Louisiana*, 391 U.S. 145, 147-50 (1968). The Supreme Court has never decided whether the Second Amendment is "incorporated," and courts have continued to apply the holdings in *Cruikshank* and *Presser*. See, e.g., *Quilici v. Village of Morton Grove*, 695 F.2d 261 (7th Cir. 1982), cert. denied, 464 U.S. 863 (1983); *Love v. Pepersack*, 47 F.3d 120 (4th Cir.), cert. denied, 516 U.S. 813 (1995). The case before this Court, however, involves a federal statute, which renders *Cruikshank* and *Presser* (and lower court decisions, like *Quilici* and *Love*, that follow their holdings) simply irrelevant.

A. The *Miller* decision.

In *United States v. Miller*, two men were indicted for violating the National Firearms Act of 1934 by transporting an unregistered short-barreled (or sawed-off) shotgun across state lines. The District Court quashed the indictment, holding without explanation that the statute was inconsistent with the Second Amendment. The government appealed to the Supreme Court, which ruled for the government without hearing any argument on behalf of the defendants.

The *Miller* opinion is short and cryptic, and its holding must be interpreted narrowly. Most of the Court's opinion is devoted to a discussion of the Framers' understanding of the militia, which the Court characterized as "civilians primarily, soldiers on occasion." 307 U.S. at 179. Without raising any question as to whether the defendants in the case were members of the militia, the Court rested its holding on the presumed nature of sawed-off shotguns:

In the absence of any evidence tending to show that possession or use of a 'shotgun having a barrel of less than eighteen inches in length' at this time has some reasonable relationship to the preservation or efficiency of a well regulated militia, we cannot say that the Second Amendment guarantees the right to keep and bear such an instrument. Certainly it is not within judicial notice that this weapon is any part of the ordinary military equipment or that its use could contribute to the common defense. *Aymette v. State of Tennessee*, 2 Humph., Tenn., 154, 158.

Id. at 178. This statement of the holding is both tentative and indefinite. The Court does not say that short-barreled shotguns fall outside the Second Amendment, but only that the Court has not been provided with a persuasive reason to regard them as protected. The Court does not say that military weapons alone are protected by the Second Amendment, but only that protected weapons must at least have some ability to contribute to "the common defense." The Court does not say that "the common defense" comprehends only foreign invaders, thus allowing for the usefulness of privately owned firearms against domestic insurrections, for ordinary law enforcement, and for self-defense against criminal attacks. And perhaps most important, the Court never embraces the erroneous suggestion, repeatedly suggested by the government in this case, that the "militia" means a military organization like the National Guard.

B. *Miller* accepted the individual right interpretation of the Second Amendment.

Miller clearly, if implicitly, acknowledged that the Second Amendment protects the individual right of citizens to keep and bear arms. This is clear from the face of the Court's opinion, which never asked whether the defendants in that case were members of the National Guard, or of the militia. Nor did the Court suggest that defendants' status as members of the militia would have had the slightest bearing on the outcome of the case. As the Justices saw it, the only issue in the case was whether the defendants had a right to possess a particular type of weapon in violation of a federal registration requirement. Furthermore, the Court remanded the case, thereby offering the defendants an opportunity to provide evidence demonstrating exactly what the Supreme Court had been unwilling to take judicial notice of: that short-barreled shotguns "could contribute to the common defense."[5]

Nor can it be supposed that the Court somehow overlooked the possibility that Second Amendment rights belong only to members of the National Guard or the militia. On the contrary, the government's brief (the only brief filed in *Miller*) specifically, repeatedly, and forcefully argued that the right to arms applies only to members of military organizations. See Brief of the United States, *Miller* (No. 696), at 4-5, 12, 15, 16. The Supreme Court refused to accept the government's argument.

C. *Miller*'s holding applies only to weapons peculiarly adapted to criminal purposes.

The *Miller* opinion must be read cautiously and narrowly, in part because some of its language seems to carry implications that the Court could not have intended. The last sentence in the quotation set forth above, for example, appears to assume that private possession of weapons that constitute "any part of the ordinary military equipment" is per se protected by the Second Amendment. In 1939, this would have included fully automatic rifles, mortars, and bazookas. Indeed, as the First Circuit pointed out shortly thereafter, it would have to include the sawed-off shotguns at issue in *Miller* itself, as well as almost any gun except militarily useless antique weapons like flintlock muskets. *Cases v. United States*, 131 F.2d 916, 922 (1942), cert. denied, 319 U.S. 770 (1943).

Reading *Miller* in light of the facts of the case, as one must, it is clear that the Court meant its holding to extend no farther than the National Firearms Act itself extended, namely to the regulation of short-barreled shotguns and rifles, machine guns, and si-

---

[5] The disposition of the case on remand is not reported.

lencers. These devices have only one characteristic in common. They appear to be particularly well-suited to criminal uses, and ill-suited to legitimate civilian purposes. This, at any rate, is certainly the view that Congress adopted, and to which the *Miller* Court provisionally deferred.[6]

We know this, first, because the government's brief in Miller strongly emphasized that the National Firearms Act was directed at weapons that "clearly have no legitimate use in the hands of private individuals but, on the contrary frequently constitute the arsenal of the gangster and the desperado." Brief for the United States, *Miller* (No. 696), at 5; see also id. at 7-8 (extensive excerpt from legislative history discussing "gangster" use of machine guns); 8 ("weapons which are the tools of the criminal"); 18 ("weapons which are commonly used by criminals"); 20 ("arsenal of the 'public enemy' and the 'gangster'").

In addition, the "criminal's weapon" theory is the only way to make sense of the *Miller* Court's otherwise inapposite citation to the Tennessee Supreme Court's opinion in *Aymette v. State*. See *Miller*, 307 U.S. at 178 (quoted above). The Tennessee court, which was construing a state constitutional provision that had a substantially different wording from the Second Amendment, could hardly have provided authority for any general interpretation of the Second Amendment. The only reason *Aymette* might have been relevant to the *Miller* case is that it dealt with certain knives that the Tennessee court said were "usually employed in private broils, and which are efficient only in the hands of the robber and the assassin." It is no accident that this language, which was quoted in the government's *Miller* Brief, at 19, occurs on exactly the page of *Aymette* cited by the Supreme Court in *Miller*. Compare 307 U.S. at 178 (quoted above) with *Aymette*, 2 Humphr. (Tenn.) at 156.

---

[6] One must characterize this deference to Congress as provisional because *Miller* said only that it was "not within judicial notice" that short-barreled shotguns were weapons of the type that would be protected under the Second Amendment. 307 U.S. at 178.

Under *Miller*, Congress may protect the public safety with measures designed to prevent criminals from acquiring weapons that are especially well suited to criminal purposes and that have few legitimate civilian purposes. The statute at issue in *Miller* involved plausible examples of such weapons (sawed-off shotguns and rifles, machine guns, and silencers), and the statute placed relatively limited obstacles (registration and a tax) in the path of the civilian who might have a genuine and legitimate need for such weapons. *Miller*, 307 U.S. at 175 n.1 (quoting National Firearms Act). Whatever *Miller* may imply about more stringent regulation of such weapons, no reasonable reading of *Miller* can possibly justify the government's current effort to impose a complete firearms disability on any citizen who becomes subject to a routine divorce court restraining order, unsupported by any finding of past or future dangerousness.

III. THE FIFTH CIRCUIT PRECEDENTS CITED BY THE GOVERNMENT DO NOT ADDRESS THE ISSUE IN THIS CASE.

Contrary to the government's startling assertions about stare decisis, this case differs fundamentally from *United States v. Johnson*, 441 F.2d 1134 (5th Cir. 1971), and *United States v. Williams*, 446 F.2d 486 (5th Cir. 1971). Both *Johnson* and *Williams* involved prosecutions for unlawful possession of an unregistered sawed-off shotgun, which was exactly the same issue decided by the Supreme Court in *Miller*. Faced with cases indistinguishable from *Miller*, this Court adhered to stare decisis and decided them the same way the Supreme Court had decided *Miller*.

Stare decisis has no bearing on a case involving a statute utterly different from the statute at issue in *Miller*, *Johnson*, and *Williams*. As we have explained, *Miller* should not, indeed cannot, be read to encompass a total firearms disability imposed without any finding of future dangerousness. The government's contention that *Johnson* and *Williams* control this case is simply insupportable.

IV. PRECEDENT FROM OTHER CIRCUITS PROVIDES NO PERSUASIVE REASON TO ACCEPT THE GOVERNMENT'S ATTEMPTED APPLICATION OF § 922(g)(8).

Several post-*Miller* decisions in other circuits have variously, and often erroneously, interpreted both the Second Amendment and *Miller*. One line of cases adopts a theory under which Second Amendment rights belong only to state governments. Modern scholarship has repeatedly demolished this theory, which has no basis whatsoever in Supreme Court precedent. In a different series of cases, courts have reached essentially the same conclusion through a far-fetched reading of *Miller*, under which it is impossible for private citizens ever to meet the requirements for Second Amendment protection of their rights.

A. The "states' right" theory should not be adopted by this Court.

The leading case for the "states' right" theory, according to which the Second Amendment does not protect any individual right, is *United States v. Tot*, 131 F.2d 261 (3rd Cir. 1942) (upholding statutory ban on possession of firearms by violent felons), reversed on other grounds, 319 U.S. 463 (1943). The *Tot* court's entire analysis, which is sheer dicta, reads as follows:

It is abundantly clear both from the discussions of this amendment contemporaneous with its proposal and adoption and those of learned writers since[13] that this amendment, unlike those providing for protection of free speech and freedom of religion, was not adopted with individual rights in mind, but as a protection for the States in the maintenance of their militia organizations against possible encroachments by the federal power.[14] The experiences in England under James II of an armed royal force quartered upon a defenseless citizenry[15] was fresh in the minds of the Colonists. They wanted no repetition of that experience in their newly formed government. The almost uniform course of decision in this country,[16] where provisions similar in language are found in many of the State Constitutions, bears out this concept of the constitutional guarantee. A notable instance is the refusal to extend its application to weapons thought incapable of military use.

13 1 Elliot's Debates on the Federal Constitution (2d Ed. 1901) 371, 372 (Luther Martin's letter to the Maryland Legislature); 4 Id. 203 (Lenoir, North Carolina Convention); 5 Id. 445 (Sherman of Connecticut at the Federal Convention). Emery, The Constitutional Right to Keep and Bear Arms (1915) 28 Harv.L.Rev. 473; Haight, The Right to Keep and Bear Arms (1941) 2 Bill of Rights Rev. 31; McKenna, The Right to Keep and Bear Arms (1928) 12 Marq.L.Rev. 138.

14 As to the latter, see The Federalist, Nos. XXIV-XXIX and No. XLVI.

15 See Aymette v. State, 1840, 2 Humph. 154, 21 Tenn. 154; also law review articles in fn. 13.

16 See Haight, supra and McKenna, supra.

131 F.2d at 266 (footnotes in original). The Tot court could not and did not cite any Supreme Court decision supporting these claims. The Supreme Court's Miller decision, which had come only three years earlier, was clearly based on the opposite conclusion: Miller went off on the nature of short-barreled shotguns without so much as a hint that the defendants' membership vel non in the militia had any bearing on their Second Amendment claims. The Supreme Court's discussion of the nature of the firearm would obviously have been irrelevant had the Court given any credence to the "states' right" theory. And, as we observed above, the Miller Court rejected the government's vigorous advocacy of the proposition that the Second Amendment protects only "members of the state militia or other similar military organization provided by law." Brief for the United States at 5, Miller (No. 696); see also id. at 12, 15, 18-20.

Nor did the Tot court actually cite any other relevant authority. Contrary to Tot's assertion about "discussions of this amendment contemporaneous with its proposal and adoption," all of the eighteenth century sources cited by the court are discussions that took place before the Constitution itself was ratified and well before the Second Amendment was drafted or proposed. See notes 13-14 in Tot (citing Martin and Lenoir at their state ratifying conventions, Sherman at the Federal Convention, and the Federalist Papers). Obviously, these discussions did not and could not have anything at all to do with interpreting the Second Amendment. Each of the eighteenth-century discussions cited in Tot dealt with a completely different issue, namely the desire of the Anti-Federalists for strong constitutional constraints on the federal government's power to keep standing armies during peacetime, and strong guarantees of the states' ability to defend themselves militarily against a potentially tyrannical federal government. The Tot Court's dicta rest on the assumption that the Second Amendment was intended to satisfy these Anti-Federalist demands by erecting "a protection for the States in the maintenance of their militia organizations against possible encroachment by the federal power." 131 F.2d at 266. This is demonstrably false, both as a matter of history and because it entails the absurd assumption that the Second Amendment repealed the provisions in Article I of the Constitution that give the federal government plenary control over the militia and that forbid the states from keeping troops without the consent of Congress. U.S. Const. art. I, § 8, cls. 15-16; § 10, cl. 3.

The Tot theory of the Second Amendment is impossible to reconcile with the text of the Constitution, and there is no historical evidence that anyone ever dreamed of such a theory until long after the founding generation had gone to their graves. The early constitutional commentators took it for granted that the Second Amendment protects the right of individuals to keep and bear arms, not some sort of states' right to maintain military forces for use against the federal government. See, e.g., St. George Tucker's edition of Blackstone's Commentaries appendix, at 300 (1803);

William Rawle, A View of the Constitution of the United States of America 153-54 (2d ed. 1829); 3 Joseph Story, Commentaries on the Constitution of the United States 746-47 (1833); Thomas M. Cooley, The General Principles of Constitutional Law in the United States of America 281-83 (2d ed. 1891).[7]

Although the states' right theory was mere dictum in Tot, see 131 F.2d at 266-67 (holding based on the government's interest in denying weapons to those who "have previously, by due process of law, been shown to be aggressors against society"), some courts have subsequently relied on the theory in deciding cases. See, e.g., United States v. Stevens, 440 F.2d 144 (6th Cir. 1971) (possession of firearm by convicted felon), overruled on other grounds, United States v. Bass, 404 U.S. 336 (1971); United States v. Johnson, 497 F.2d 548 (4th Cir. 1974) (interstate transportation of firearm by a convicted felon); United States v. Warin, 530 F.2d 103 (6th Cir. 1976) (possession of unregistered machine gun), cert. denied, 426 U.S. 948 (1976); Hickman v. Block, 81 F.3d 98 (9th Cir.) (state government's refusal to issue permit to carry a concealed handgun), cert. denied, 519 U.S. 912 (1996). Not a single one of these opinions makes the slightest effort to respond to the enormous textual and historical difficulties entailed in the Tot dicta. Hickman and Warin merely cite prior cases that adopted the states' right theory. Johnson and Stevens, even more egregiously, purport to rely on Miller, a case in which the Supreme Court had actually refused to adopt the states' right theory.

Furthermore, none of these cases involved the kind of sweeping and arbitrary firearms disability created by the government's application of § 922(g)(8) in this case. All of these courts could have upheld the statutes at issue without recourse to the untenable states' right theory, and their decisions provide no reason at all for this Court to adopt that hollow and

---

[7] Nor did any court adopt the states' right theory until the twentieth century. The first such decisions were *Salina v. Blakesley*, 83 P. 619 (Kan. 1905), and *United States v. Adams*, 11 F. Supp. 216 (S.D. Fla. 1935).

misguided interpretation of the Second Amendment.

B. This Court should not adopt an interpretation of *Miller* that renders the Second Amendment a dead letter.

A distinct line of cases has read Miller to put insurmountable hurdles in the path of any citizen who asserts his or her Second Amendment rights to keep and bear arms. These cases misinterpret Miller to mean that Second Amendment rights can only be exercised in the context of military service. As explained above, Miller only becomes coherent when read as a decision about regulating weapons that are useful primarily to criminals. Furthermore, each of the circuit court opinions that adopts a broad and loose reading of Miller could have reached the same result through a more restrained application of the Supreme Court's guidance. Indeed, all of the cases discussed below are essentially indistinguishable from the Supreme Court's decision in Miller because they involve the very same weapons regulated by the statute at issue in Miller itself.[8]

The leading decision is Cases v. United States, 131 F.2d 916 (1st Cir. 1942), which upheld a federal statute imposing a firearms disability on persons convicted of a violent crime. After noting the nonsensical consequences entailed in Miller's apparent assumption that the Second Amendment protects the civilian possession of military weapons, and military weapons alone, Cases essentially declared the Second Amendment unintelligible:

Considering the many variable factors bearing

---

[8] Other cases cited by the government involved statutes imposing firearms disabilities where there has been a judicial finding of past or future misconduct. *See United States v. Friel*, 1 F.3d 1231 (1st Cir. 1993) (upholding federal felon-in-possession statute); *Gillespie v. City of Indianapolis*, 185 F.3d 693 (7th Cir. 1999) (upholding federal statute imposing firearms disability as a consequence of criminal conviction for domestic violence). These decisions therefore offer no support for the government's radical claim that a firearms disability may be imposed without any finding of misconduct or dangerousness.

upon the question it seems to us impossible to formu-
late any general test by which to determine the limits
imposed by the Second Amendment but that each case
under it, like cases under the due process clause,
must be decided on its own facts and the line between
what is and what is not a valid federal restriction
pricked out by decided cases falling on one side or the
other of the line.

Id. at 922. In a remarkably confused application of
this common law approach to the Second Amendment,
the court then sustained the defendant's conviction on
the ground that he did not belong to a military organization, was not using the gun "in preparation for
a military career," and was acting "without any
thought or intention of contributing to the efficiency of
the well regulated militia." Id. at 923. This seems to
imply that violent felons would be entitled to possess
firearms if they were "preparing" for a military career,
or perhaps even if they were careful to think of themselves as "militia men" while carrying their guns
about. This is every bit as nonsensical as the interpretation of Miller from which the Cases court itself un-
derstandably recoiled. It is certainly not a correct interpretation of Miller.

Several subsequent courts have proceeded in the
same rudderless fashion. Like Cases, each of these
decisions involved statutes that could easily have
been upheld on narrow and readily defensible
grounds, for they involved virtually the same facts as
those at issue in Miller itself. See, e.g., United States
v. Wright, 117 F.3d 1265 (11th Cir. 1997) (possession
of unregistered machine guns), cert. denied, 118 S. Ct.
584 (1997); United States v. Rybar, 103 F.3d 273 (3d
Cir. 1996) (same), cert. denied, 118 S. Ct. 46 (1997);
United States v. Hale, 978 F.2d 1016 (8th Cir. 1992)
(same), cert. denied, 507 U.S. 997 (1993); United
States v. Oakes, 564 F.2d 384 (10th Cir. 1977) (same),
cert. denied, 435 U.S. 926 (1978).[9] Unfortunately and
unnecessarily, these courts have adopted sweeping

---

[9] *See also United States v. Toner*, 728 F.2d 115 (2d Cir. 1984) (equal-
protection challenge to statute requiring registration of machine guns).

rationales that essentially render the Second Amendment a dead letter.

Thus, for example, Rybar somehow read Miller's reference to "a reasonable relationship to the preservation or efficiency of a well-regulated militia," to imply that the Second Amendment does not cover those who are in fact members of the militia of the United States. 103 F.3d at 286. Similarly, Wright and Oakes somehow read Miller to mean that the Second Amendment does not cover those who are in fact members of their state militia. 117 F.3d at 1273; 564 F.2d at 387. Hale seems to have concluded that the Second Amendment is for all practical purposes merely a piece of "historical residue." 978 F.2d at 1019.

The common thread in all these opinions is the notion that Second Amendment rights belong only to those whom the government has included in its formal military organizations. This simply turns the Constitution upside down, converting a protected constitutional right into a privilege that the government is free to bestow or withhold at will. As Justice Cooley cogently noted over a century ago:

> [T]he militia, as has been elsewhere explained, consists of those persons who, under the law, are liable to the performance of military duty, and are officered and enrolled for service when called upon. But the law may make provision for the enrolment of all who are fit to perform military duty, or of a small number only, or it may wholly omit to make any provision at all; and if the right [to keep and bear arms] were limited to those enrolled, the purpose of this guaranty might be defeated altogether by the action or neglect to act of the government it was meant to hold in check. The meaning of the provision undoubtedly is, that the people, from whom the militia must be taken, shall have the right to keep and bear arms, and they need no permission or regulation of law for the purpose.

Thomas M. Cooley, The General Principles of Constitutional Law in the United States of America 282 (2d ed. 1891) (emphasis added). This Court should decline to follow the Cases line of decisions, which is based on a plain distortion of Miller and on an utterly untenable interpretation of the Constitution.

CONCLUSION

No court has ever upheld a federal statute that entails the kind of sweeping and unjustified infringement of Second Amendment rights involved in the government's application of § 922(g)(8). The District Court correctly rejected the government's attempt to assume these unnecessary and dangerous new powers. The constitutional analysis of the court below is fully supported by the constitutional text and constitutional history, and it is not foreclosed by any precedent binding on this Court. Accordingly, the judgment below should be AFFIRMED.

Quantity Discounts

Gun Rights Affirmed

Give a copy to everyone you know!

Now is the time to get this book into the hands of every American. Order 25, 50, or 100 copies. Send them to your friends. Give them to business associates. Mail one to everyone you know.

DISCOUNT SCHEDULE

1 copy	$10.00	25 copies	$175.00
5 copies	$45.00	50 copies	$300.00
10 copies	$85.00	100 copies	$500.00
	500 copies	$2,000	

ORDER YOURS TODAY!

Merril Press
PO Box 1682
Bellevue, WA 98009

Please send me _____ copies of **GUN RIGHTS AFFIRMED**.
Enclosed is a check or money order for $_____.

Please charge my ☐ **VISA** ☐ **MasterCard** ☐ **AMEX** ☐ **Discover**

Number _____ **Expires**_____
Signature _____
Name _____
Street _____
City_____ **State** _____**Zip** _____
Phone (_____)_____ Email_____@_____

Quantity Discounts

Gun Rights Affirmed

Give a copy to everyone you know!

Now is the time to get this book into the hands of every American. Order 25, 50, or 100 copies. Send them to your friends. Give them to business associates. Mail one to everyone you know.

DISCOUNT SCHEDULE

1 copy	$10.00	25 copies	$175.00
5 copies	$45.00	50 copies	$300.00
10 copies	$85.00	100 copies	$500.00
	500 copies	$2,000	

ORDER YOURS TODAY!

Merril Press
PO Box 1682
Bellevue, WA 98009

Please send me _____ copies of **GUN RIGHTS AFFIRMED**.
Enclosed is a check or money order for $_____.

Please charge my ☐ **VISA** ☐ **MasterCard** ☐ **AMEX** ☐ **Discover**

Number _____ **Expires**_____

Signature _____

Name _____

Street _____

City_____ **State** _____**Zip** _____

Phone (____)_____ **Email**_____@_____

Quantity Discounts

Gun Rights Affirmed

Give a copy to everyone you know!

Now is the time to get this book into the hands of every American. Order 25, 50, or 100 copies. Send them to your friends. Give them to business associates. Mail one to everyone you know.

DISCOUNT SCHEDULE

1 copy	$10.00	25 copies	$175.00
5 copies	$45.00	50 copies	$300.00
10 copies	$85.00	100 copies	$500.00
	500 copies		$2,000

ORDER YOURS TODAY!

Merril Press
PO Box 1682
Bellevue, WA 98009

Please send me _____ copies of **GUN RIGHTS AFFIRMED**. Enclosed is a check or money order for $_____.

Please charge my ☐ **VISA** ☐ **MasterCard** ☐ **AMEX** ☐ **Discover**

Number _____ **Expires**_____
Signature _____
Name _____
Street _____
City_____ **State** _____**Zip** _____
Phone (_____**)**_____ **Email**_____**@**_____